THE COLOUR OF WINE

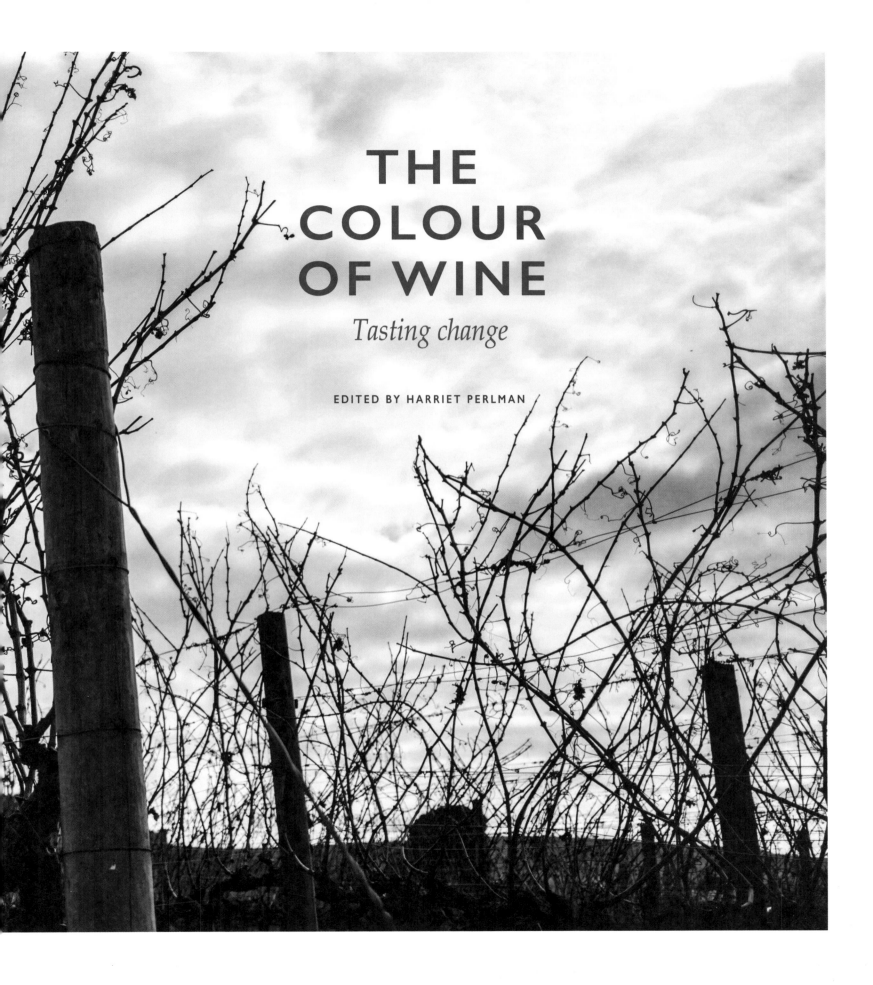

THE COLOUR OF WINE

Tasting change

EDITED BY HARRIET PERLMAN

© Kalipha Foundation, 2018

This book was made possible by the generous funding of the Kalipha Foundation of Mion Holdings.

ISBN: 978-1-928333-10-4
e-ISBN: 978-1-928333-11-1

First edition, first impression 2018

Published on behalf of the Kalipha Foundation of Mion Holdings by
Rainbird, an imprint of Bookstorm (Pty) Ltd

Kalipha Foundation
77 Old Main Road
Botha's Hill 3660
KwaZulu-Natal

Compiler and editor: Harriet Perlman
Photo editor: Mark Lewis
Writers: Sharon Cort, Jaci de Villiers, Wesley Thompson, John Platter, Michelle Hay, Michael Fridjhon
Photographs:
Mark Lewis: cover, 6, 10, 12, 15, 18, 20, 23, 24, 27, 28, 32, 34, 37, 42, 51 (ii), 80, 83, 84, 89, 96, 105, 107, 108, 112, 121, 123, 124, 126, 129, 130, 132, 134, 136, 138, 140, 143, 144, 146, 148, 150, 151, 155, 157, 160
Victor Dlamini: 9, 40, 50, 51 (i), 74, 75, 78, 79, 87, 91, 93, 95, 99, 115, 116, 152, 154, 158
Clinton Basson: back cover, 3, 17, 70, 73 (i, iv), 76
Christopher Grant Harvey: 45, 46 (i, iii, vi), 52, 73 (vi)
Marc Baleiza: 46 (ii, iv, v), 49, 54, 73 (ii, iii, v)
Cover photograph: Unathi Mantshongo (model)
AAM Archives: 62
Africa Media Online: 65, 111
Associated Press: 100 (AP/Dennis Farrell)
Bailey's African History Archives: 60
Gallo: 67, (i) Gallo/Foto24/Lulama Zenzile; (ii) Gallo/The Times/Shelley Christians;
(iii) Reuters/Mike Hutchings; (iv) Gallo; (v) Gallo/Foto24/Lulama Zenzile
Shutterstock: 57
Chefs: Nompumelelo Mqwebu, Marsel Janse van Rensburg, Sithembiso Mthethwa
Editor: Tracey Hawthorne
Proofreader: Wesley Thompson
Cover designer: René de Wet
Book design and typesetting: René de Wet
Printed by ABC Press, Cape Town

CONTENTS

INTRODUCTION

Harriet Perlman

The Colour of Wine isn't just another book about picturesque Cape vineyards. Instead, it tells the remarkable story of South Africa's transition from apartheid to democracy through the personal journeys of black winemakers. Woven through their stories are interviews with wine producers and politicians, chefs and sommeliers, connoisseurs and teachers.

Ntsiki Biyela, Dumisani Mathonsi and Unathi Mantshongo share their journeys from the remote villages and small towns where they grew up to the competitive and once exclusively white world of wine. As youngsters, they never tasted wine, let alone imagined a career in making it, but opportunities presented themselves and they grabbed them with both hands. They were among the first black students to study at Stellenbosch University – historically one of the bastions of Afrikaner nationalism.

Carmen Stevens, however, always wanted to be a winemaker. Growing up on the Cape Flats, with a mother who tried to keep her away from wine, Carmen, like her winemaking colleagues, battled prejudice and other challenges. However, with humour and courage, and the support of mentors and teachers, they have all carved remarkable careers in the wine industry.

The Colour of Wine also explores the history of wine in South Africa. Dating back to the first white settlers in the mid-1600s, it's an industry built on slave labour and racial discrimination. Prior to 1994, there were few black South African consumers of wine and even fewer black wine producers. The industry, once dominated by a small elite and wealthy white minority, has seen remarkable changes in the 24 years since the dawn of democracy – but whether these changes have been extensive enough is a matter of heated debate.

In a thoughtful contribution, John Platter, regarded by many as a doyen of South African wine, looks back – and forwards – offering fresh insights into where we are now and where the industry needs to go.

South Africa exported 25 million litres of wine in 1993; by 2014 this figure had ballooned to a staggering 500 million litres worldwide. But this expansion in the export wine market has not been matched in domestic consumption. One of the biggest challenges facing the South African wine industry is how to develop a domestic consumer base. In a country dominated by beer drinkers, wine merchants such as Mnikelo Mangciphu are trying to change that, providing a space for people not only to buy wine but to learn about it too.

Most would agree that wine and food go together. South Africa has a rich food culture that stretches across different traditions and heritages. You'll find a delicious array of local recipes to complement local wines. Bongani Ngwenya, a sommelier at a top Johannesburg restaurant, gives his views on pairing food and wine. He left Newcastle in KwaZulu-Natal for the Cape as a young boy because he couldn't find work, and got his first job grooming and feeding horses on a wine estate. Chef Nompumelelo Mqwebu shares her journey from Umlazi township, where she grew up, to representing South African food in Germany and France. Her recipes are a celebration of African cuisine.

The Colour of Wine highlights the emergence of black winemakers, entrepreneurs and producers, and shines a light on the birth of democracy and the challenges of change. It gives a taste of the new world of wine in South Africa today.

PREVIOUS SPREAD:
Rowena Setle, Morara Wine.
OPPOSITE: *On the set of*
The Colour of Wine
documentary film, Soweto.

MAKING WINE

DUMISANI MATHONSI

FROM HERDING CATTLE TO MAKING WINE

I would never have thought that I'd end up making wine. I'd seen wine on shop shelves, and from time to time I drank cheap sweet wine, after a sports event or at weddings or parties in the village.

I grew up in the small village of Hluhluwe, on the north coast of KwaZulu-Natal. My mother raised us because my father worked in Johannesburg, but he came home often.

We were a very close family. My aunt ran a crèche to keep us out of trouble. My good relationship with teachers started there because my aunt loved me and praised me to my parents.

I attended local schools until I matriculated at 16. I was always the boy the teachers trusted. If they needed anything done, they would ask me to do it.

Like most rural boys, when I wasn't at school I helped to herd the cattle and plough the fields. I remember on Monday mornings we had to get up very early and walk ten kilometres to help dip the cattle before going to school. My peers respected me and followed my lead. I really enjoyed school and I had a very good herd.

I was the top student in my high school but I had no idea what I wanted to do after school. I would never have thought that I'd end up making wine. I'd seen wine on shop shelves, and from time to time I drank cheap sweet wine, after a sports event or at weddings or parties in the village. I had no idea where it came from or that it was made from grapes.

Then, in my matric year, the [then] KwaZulu-Natal Minister of Education, Eileen KaNkosi-Shandu, came to talk to us about her friend in the wine industry, Jabulani Ntshangase, who wanted to recruit students to apply for a bursary to study winemaking. My teachers had been helping me to apply for bursaries to study engineering at a technikon. After Mam Shandu's visit they encouraged me to study viticulture (grape-growing) and oenology (winemaking) at Stellenbosch University. I received a bursary. It was a great opportunity for me and I grabbed it with both hands.

We grew up thinking Cape Town was the furthest place you could go. It was like a foreign country. My teachers were incredibly helpful in organising my long journey to Stellenbosch. It was on and off buses and into taxis.

Seeing Stellenbosch for the first time was quite a shock. It was so different to where I came from. It was so neat and laid back. I thought it was beautiful and I still do.

I met some other students on the way. When I asked one of them how she was finding Stellenbosch, she answered that she was 'coping'. I had no idea what that meant and had to look it up in the dictionary.

I was always very comfortable in my own skin so I wasn't that worried about going there. Also, one of my teachers who'd studied at Stellenbosch put me at ease by saying that if I was disciplined I would be fine.

When we arrived in Cape Town, the Retief family were there to meet us and take us to Jabulani Ntshangase's house in Stellenbosch. He was so warm and welcoming that it felt like a home away from home.

Jabulani put four of us up at his other house in Malmesbury. In registration week he would drive us to Stellenbosch through the Swartland. He was passionate about the area and this was a chance for him to talk about the vineyards and winemaking. We started to get a feel for the area and what it was all about.

The first day of registration was a shock. One of the ladies told me that I was going to be lectured in Afrikaans. I was terrified. I went back to Jabulani and said, 'Is this correct, what I'm hearing? It's hard enough for me to come and study something I have no idea about and on top of that I'm going to be lectured in Afrikaans!' Then we found out that if we attended BSc Forestry classes we could do the same classes in English. That eased a lot of pressure because once you're through your first year, your second and third years actually become easier. You're more familiar with the environment and have acclimatised.

Living with Jabulani was great. I had no experience of eating out but Jabulani took us to restaurants. We sat and discussed wine but we didn't really drink at that time. Jabulani believed that to have a healthy mind, you had to have a healthy body. He had us up every morning at 6am and we would go for a long run. By the time we got to our classes we were very fresh and awake. Even when Jabulani was in New York, he would phone early every morning to check that we were up and running. He knew we were teenagers and we were naughty.

In third and fourth year, all the classes were in Afrikaans. It was weird because even the jokes were in Afrikaans. People were laughing but we didn't know what they were laughing about. We couldn't participate. Luckily, the lecturers were very accommodating.

I made sure I never missed a class, even if it was in Afrikaans. This made my life easier because the lecturers were even more willing to help me.

In October of my first year I got a place at a residence closer to the university. It was more convenient for me at lunchtimes and when I wanted to go to the library. Also, before that, the police would often stop me walking on the street and check my bags. I felt harassed by them.

TOP LEFT: *Dumisani with his mother, Mamnyandu Mathonsi.*
TOP RIGHT: *Dumisani with his siblings from left, Mondli, Shongaziphi and Mlayezo (standing).*
CENTRE RIGHT: *Mama Mhlongo, local shop owner.*

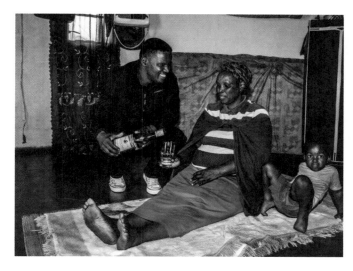

I started doing things that boys at res do, like partying and going to clubs and dancing. I stopped my early-morning runs but I went to gym in the evenings with the other boys and then studied when we got back. Sometimes we had a drink or two in the evening.

The highlight of my student life was when I was first introduced to oenology. My lecturer saw some potential in me and organised for me to do practical work at Rustenberg Estate. It was encouraging to know that someone was interested in helping me achieve what I wanted to achieve. My work there gave me a lot of confidence because I'd never worked in a vineyard before. I'd ride through the vineyards on a bicycle, learning first-hand about things like planting, how to train young vines, and vine spacing.

I met Adi Badenhorst, the winemaker there. He's a fantastic guy. He's a maverick and a hands-on winemaker. He was always the first to arrive, at 6am, in his shorts and T-shirt, just working like everyone else. When we received barrels he'd help us offload them. If I didn't wash a barrel properly, he'd roll it back to me to rewash without saying anything bad. I got my work ethic from him.

From the moment I first walked into a winery, I got excited about winemaking. I loved the set-up of the wine cellars and the conditions: that beautiful smell of fresh yeast, taking samples of fresh fermenting juice, those aromatic flavours of cultivar Sauvignon Blancs as you walk in fresh in the morning. I was blown away. The passion that winemakers have kind of gets into you. I started seeing what my life would be like, from the vineyard to the cellar.

When I went back to university and they talked about a pump, I'd seen a pump. When they talked about a crusher, I'd seen a crusher.

I wasn't scared. I interacted and asked questions. I earned the respect of my lecturers and the other students, who were mostly Afrikaans. At our end-of-year function before graduation, we wrote things about each other on pieces of paper. I got one that said 'most likely to succeed'. I'm very shy and found it strange but it helped me to move forward.

My graduation was a huge achievement for me. When I first went to university, my parents didn't know what I was going to study but they were very proud of me. My father came to witness my graduation.

I already had a job to go to Tokara, a prestigious winery. I was overwhelmed with the amount of responsibility and pressure this meant. I remember when I was going to the interview, I called my father and said, 'Dad, I have to go to this interview and I don't want to make a fool of myself. What do I know about wine?'

On the morning of the interview I called the agent and said, 'Don't pick me up. I've decided to go back to varsity to get more years of experience.' She encouraged me, saying I was a good candidate and it was a great opportunity.

Miles Mossop, the winemaker at Tokara, phoned. He said, 'Dumisani, I understand you want to go back to university and carry on your studies but I just want to meet you and talk to you about this position.' He came to my res and took me to see the winery. In the end, I said yes to the job.

Coming to Tokara was just the beginning. Forget the college and the university education. You only learn to appreciate wine when you work with the product. I worked at Tokara for 14 years as the assistant winemaker. In 2017 I was appointed the white-winemaker at Adam Tas Cellars.

'From the moment I first walked into a winery, I got excited about winemaking. I loved the set-up of the wine cellars and the conditions: that beautiful smell of fresh yeast.'

*Dumisani's homestead in the village of
eNtombigezile in KwaZulu-Natal.*

CARMEN STEVENS

NOTHING ON A SILVER PLATE

I love that people love to drink my wine. Every winemaker puts her own personality into a wine, and if people enjoy your wine, they're enjoying you as the person you are.

I grew up in Kraaifontein in Cape Town, until my parents got divorced when I was near the end of primary school. My siblings and I moved to Belhar on the Cape Flats with my mother. We only saw our father every now and then.

My mother was the most important person in my life. She was a religious person. She was very protective of us, especially the girls. Belhar was notorious for gangsterism so my mother decided that my sister and I should continue our schooling in Kraaifontein. Rival gangs were always looking for my brother and home wasn't a safe place. My mother was always frightened the family would be attacked.

In 1995 tragedy befell our family when my brother was killed in gang violence. During that year my sister and I were living at college and only went home on weekends and holidays. It was my mother's way of protecting us. In a strange way, after his death my mother could almost breathe again, and not be scared of who would come knocking on the door.

Already in primary school I'd decided that I wanted to be a winemaker. I was really bad at writing and reading English and my mother didn't know what to do any more. She loved reading Mills & Boon and she said, 'Try this.' I was in Standard 2. I didn't understand half of it but it intrigued me. I fell in love with the romantic settings of vineyards, cellars and wine.

In my second-last year of high school I began researching how I could follow my dream. Nobody in my community knew anything about it. Through a friend's uncle I managed to get a tour of the Stellenbosch Farmers' Winery and found out that I could study winemaking at Elsenburg Agricultural Training Institute. *Fantastic,* I thought. I had no idea of the difficult years that lay ahead of me.

When I was in matric in 1990, I applied to Elsenburg but was rejected on the grounds that I wasn't white. My mother suggested I should go for teaching. After three days at teachers' college I decided I didn't want to be a teacher. I wanted to be in the wine industry. I wanted to make wine.

I reapplied to Elsenburg. My mother wouldn't be able to pay for me so I took on all sorts of jobs. I cleaned houses. I took the money I had made and bought shoes, which I sold at Cape Town Station. I also made Easter eggs and chocolate clusters, which my mother sold at the Salt River factory where she worked. My mother was very supportive because she wanted my sister and me to be educated so that we would be independent women. She didn't want us to struggle like she had as a woman on her own.

Elsenburg rejected me again, on the grounds that I had no agricultural experience and hadn't done military training!

Then one day I was paging through *Huisgenoot* and saw that Lyceum, a correspondence college, was offering a one-year agricultural course. I enrolled immediately. When I did well in my first exams, I went straight to the Elsenburg Institute and said, 'This is the third time I'm applying. I'm now studying agriculture, and if you reject me again, I'm going to the newspapers.'

I was accepted and started at Elsenburg in 1993.

The first time I tasted wine was at Elsenburg. One of the third-year students came and asked our group of girls if we wanted to see the barrel cellar. The smell, the way it looked, or what I imagined from books, was exactly what I experienced. We drank from the barrels with straws. It was an amazing experience.

But being at Elsenburg was a rude awakening for me. Out of 100 students there were only five women and two black students. I nearly ran away on the first day.

A few days later, I got called over by a group of second-year students. There were ten of them. One said, 'What are you doing here?'

I said, 'What are *you* doing here?'

He answered threateningly, 'Here, I ask questions and you answer, and when you answer, you will address me as Baas.'

I said, 'That's funny because I don't recall ever working on your dad's farm.'

He said, 'So you think that you're clever. Let me assure you, Miss Stevens, you're too stupid to ever have any kind of diploma from this college.'

I walked away and thought, *Is it really going to be that difficult?*

The next week, when we got our textbooks, I saw they were the same as the ones I'd used at Lyceum. I went and knocked on his door. When he opened it, I said, 'You told me that I was too stupid to ever get a diploma at Elsenburg. If this textbook is difficult for you, you must be bloody stupid.'

But I was really traumatised by the incident. Right there, I made a lot of enemies that followed me for the rest of my time at Elsenburg. I never knew people could be so heartless. These boys came from places where the farm workers spoke to them with bowed heads. I was the complete opposite of this. My dad always said, 'When you speak to people, look them in their eyes. Don't stand back for anybody. And don't ever assume that people owe you anything. Go and get what you want.'

TOP: *Carmen in Belhar on the Cape Flats, where she grew up.*
BOTTOM: *Carmen at a school feeding scheme she supports.*

Over the next 18 months, things got increasingly worse. I'd never experienced this kind of racism before. I was a nervous wreck. My mother said, 'Either you pack your bags or I'm coming to pack them and bring you home.'

Before leaving, I went to see Dr Johan Burger, the head of agriculture at Elsenburg. By the time I got to his office, I was totally paranoid. I just burst out, 'Do you know why I'm here? I'm here to tell you that I'm going to each and every newspaper in this country and I'm going to close this college down.'

He sat me down with a cup of tea and showed me a box of monthly reports about me. The reports told how well I'd integrated with the rest of the students at Elsenburg. He said I needed to try take things with a pinch of salt.

He then wanted to hear my side. I told him about the numerous times I'd laid complaints and how people made me feel that it was their territory, not mine. He offered to expel the students.

I told him that all I wanted was for them to apologise and treat me like a human being. I needed them to understand that I was at the college on merit and that it was unacceptable to treat anyone with such disrespect, that this institution wouldn't tolerate racism. So they were made to apologise and after that things got much better.

Still, when we grouped for our end-of-year class photograph, the photographer (an outsider) told me to stand aside because I wasn't part of the class. My lecturer got very upset and told him off. But that was the mentality at Elsenburg then.

Once, at a wine-tasting, a big man walked in and said, 'Carmen Stevens, please stand up.' I ignored him, thinking it was just another underhanded way of picking on me. It turned out that he was Charles Hopkins, now the winemaker at De Grendel. He'd been following my career at Elsenburg and he told me to call him if I ever needed a job. The fellow students who I'd been with for almost three years suddenly saw me in a different light. I'll always be grateful to him.

At the end of 1995, I qualified as the first black South African winemaker from Elsenburg.

Amazingly, I was accepted into the industry quite easily. My first job as a winemaker was at Distell's Zonnebloem Cellar. I worked incredibly hard and became a very tough winemaker. The managing director, Koos Jordaan, was like a dad and a great mentor to me.

In 1998 he arranged for me to do a harvest internship in California. When I returned to Distell I was appointed as winemaker for one of the first black-empowerment ventures in South Africa under the brand Tukulu Wines, but still under the Distell umbrella. With our maiden vintage we ranked in the top ten Pinotage. We got Lufthansa First Class and Veritas Gold. These awards opened a lot of doors for me.

But when I applied to be a white-winemaker for Distell, I was told I didn't have enough experience. I was angry, as I'd been there for five years and had worked on these wines. I applied for a winemaker position with another company, got the job and resigned from Distell.

In 2005, I got to live my dream. I took up a position as winemaker at Amani Wines. It was a small cellar and I had carte blanche. It was really great experience.

'My dad always said, "When you speak to people, look them in their eyes. Don't stand back for anybody. And don't ever assume that people owe you anything. Go and get what you want." '

One evening in February 2010, I got an unexpected call. A man introduced himself and asked, 'How would you like to have your own wine label?' He had a very posh English accent and I thought it was a prank call.

I said, 'It's Friday night. Don't you have something better to do? Where did you get my number and who put you up to this?' I thought it was too good to be true.

I then discovered the call was from Rowan Gormley, the founder of Naked Wines, an online retailer. Their customers support independent winemakers in return for exclusive access to excellent wines at wholesale prices.

I felt I couldn't leave Amani as they'd been so good to me. Also, as a divorced mother of two girls, I needed something secure. But later in the year I took up the offer.

Naked Wines launched my label on their website where customers could buy my wines. The idea was to have my wines on the site for a week to see if there was interest in my brand. In the first ten hours on the first day, we'd sold over R1,2 million-worth of wine that hadn't even been bottled yet! My solo career as a winemaker had started with a bang in the UK market.

It isn't easy being a black winemaker and a woman. It's still a very white male-dominated industry. People think that because you come from a disadvantaged background, you get things on a silver plate. I didn't get anything on a plate. I've worked hard every day for 22 years. My own production has grown with the help of Naked Wines, and I also mentor and make wine for another brand, Kunjani Wines in Stellenbosch, under the name Carmen Stevens Wines.

In 2011, I started a small soup kitchen in Belhar, serving a cup of soup to 300–500 learners three times a week. Today, with the help of Naked Wines, we're providing the funds to feed learners every day they attend school. In 2018, we provided breakfast and lunch every schoolday to 5 754 learners in 28 schools in the Western Cape.

Although the scheme has expanded to other areas, the focus remains in Belhar. I come from that place and I know what it is to be hungry. I want to put something back into the community where I grew up.

UNATHI MANTSHONGO

BECOMING VISIBLE

I like that you get your hands dirty when you're growing the grapes and when you're making the wine. I like that you also get a bit of the glam once the wine is made … The first time I tasted wine was in my third year at varsity. We had to experiment and make our own wine. It tasted terrible. I couldn't believe people were drinking it. I couldn't believe it took four years to study to make something that was quite tough to swallow.

I was born in Mthatha in the Eastern Cape. I went to school there, until I was in Grade 10, when we went to live in Boksburg on the East Rand of Johannesburg, where I completed my schooling.

Growing up, the only liquor I knew about was beer. I knew nothing about wine and I definitely had never heard of winemaking as a career. In fact, I only learned how to pronounce 'oenology' when I was standing in line to register at Stellenbosch University!

I wasn't sure what I wanted to do after school, but I love being outdoors so I thought becoming a quantity surveyor would suit me. But I didn't have much choice. My mother was a single parent raising three kids and couldn't afford to put me through university.

We started searching for bursaries when I was in Grade 11. On Sundays after lunch we'd spread out the newspaper and cut out the bursaries I could apply for. My mother applied for a bursary from the Department of Agriculture, Forestry and Fisheries (DAFF) for me to study for a BSc in viticulture and oenology.

I'd applied for several other bursaries too but when I didn't hear anything from them, we decided to head to Wits university, where I'd been accepted for quantity surveying. As we hit the highway, my mom got a call. I answered because she was driving but when she heard it was from DAFF she stopped the car on the side of the highway to talk to them. They were offering me a comprehensive bursary that covered my studies, books, food and accommodation. She talked, took down notes, asked questions and made the tough decision there and then to send me to Stellenbosch to study winemaking. My mom turned the car around and we headed back to the East Rand Mall to buy me bedding for res.

When we got home my mom and I googled 'winemaking' to find out what it was all about. I still wasn't sure what I was going to be studying! My mom was more concerned than I was. She assured me that if I didn't like it, I could get a job and pay back the sponsors or graduate and study something else. I saw it as a new experience but had no idea of how much hard work was involved.

I began my undergraduate degree at Stellenbosch University in 2004. The first day at Stellenbosch was a real culture shock. My mom dropped me off at res and bought me all the res T-shirts but she had to fly back to Joburg on the same day. The moment I realised I was one of only four black kids in my first-year class, and there were only two black students at the residence where I was staying, was very sobering.

I struggled to take part in res life because I didn't know the language and it was such a different culture, from the songs you sang to celebrate scoring a goal, to the house dances and the food. It all tasted and sounded strange – I'd never eaten bobotie, and I didn't really like the sweet porridge they made with cinnamon and sugar.

I missed things from home that I'd taken for granted. I used to think of food like umngqusho and amasi as backwards, but at Stellenbosch I longed for them.

People tried to include me but I always had to get involved in *their* culture. They didn't try to get to know *my* culture, which made it difficult to adapt.

Being a black student at Stellenbosch was pretty difficult. It was almost like being invisible. But I did make some good and interesting friends there from all over the world.

It was also hard because our lectures were in Afrikaans. I think one of the funnier moments at varsity was when one of our biochemistry lecturers wanted to stress that Stellenbosch was an Afrikaans institution. She walked into our first class and told us this in Afrikaans. Ironically, most of us didn't understand what she was saying. I just saw someone getting really upset at the front of the lecture hall, and then later one of our classmates told us what she'd said. These sorts of experiences taught me not to take things personally and helped me to progress.

Not everyone was like that. There were other lecturers who took a keen interest in the black students and gave us extra lessons to make sure we were coping.

Studying winemaking was literally a new experience every day for me because I'd never even seen a vine in my life. I remember being very surprised the first time we went to the university farm. I was studying science so I wondered what we were doing farming. Then I realised that my other major was actually about growing grapes! Winemaking was really so foreign to me.

The first time I tasted wine was in my third year. We had to experiment and make our own wine. It tasted terrible. I couldn't believe people were drinking it. I couldn't believe it took four years to study to make something that was quite tough to swallow. It was only in my final year, when we got to taste some expensive wines, that I tasted something that I thought was drinkable.

My mother and I told people that I was studying agriculture because it would've been difficult to explain that she'd sent her child away for four years to study liquor. Only when I started appearing in magazines because I was a black woman working on wine farms did we tell people that I'd studied winemaking, with the disclaimer that it was 'very different to beer'.

My graduation was a highlight because it meant that my life in the way that I wanted to live it was going to start. I used to think that most black people who graduated didn't stay in winemaking. I thought that they just finished their degrees, got a job and worked themselves out of the industry as soon as they could. This was until I met Ntsiki Biyela. She was a black winemaker and Stellenbosch graduate who came to give us a talk to get us excited about winemaking. She was really inspiring. But I still didn't think I could be a winemaker.

In my fourth year, for my winemaking harvest practical, I went for a job interview at Rustenberg Estate. I walked in and told [then winemaker] Adi Badenhorst that I didn't want to be a winemaker. He asked me how much I weighed and I thought this was really rude. Then he told me that I'd be washing tanks and carrying barrels so I needed to be pretty strong. I said that I was strong in a different way – mentally. I got the job.

I had to learn to drive a four-wheeler bike so I could get to all the vineyards on the farm. I tasted a lot of grapes. I checked whether they needed water. I decided when they would be ready to be harvested. Adi also bought in quality grapes from other regions and we drove hundreds of kilometres every week. I learned to tell the difference between friendly and harmful insects.

I began to understand more about the science of growing grapes. This reinforced my love for viticulture, which had begun when I had a holiday job at Tokara. I started falling in love with the fact that you have very little control, and for all the science in the world, Mother Nature decides.

After obtaining my degree I worked as a viticulturist at KWV [Koöperatieve Wijnbouwers Vereniging, Cooperative Winemakers' Union] for four years. At first, it was quite sobering. I was a woman and I was young. I had a degree and I was working with farmers more than twice my age. At the same time, I was doing a postgraduate degree in viticulture. It was a bit of a juggle but I learned a lot from my manager and current industry colleague, Cobus van Graan. KWV is where I established myself and learned to be a professional.

When I moved to Nederburg I was in charge of all the viticulture and grape buying for the brand. I had a lot of ideas and it was very exciting to be able to implement them. I loved being involved in the actual farming of the grapes. My office was the wide expanse of vineyards. I learned a lot about the uniqueness of different vineyards all over the Cape and even the Northern Cape.

I couldn't have imagined that I'd be so happy to be part of the wine industry, I suspect working outdoors had something to do with it. There are so many things I like, like the fact that you can create something with your own hands. Working outdoors has a lot to do with it. I like that it's small, so you get to know people quite quickly and create networks. I love that you get to travel because our benchmark is international.

Now, as the CEO at the VinPro Foundation, I have to use my passion to meet the challenge of educating young people about winemaking and transforming the leadership of the wine industry. My dream is to have South Africans who are passionate about wine running South African wine businesses and seeing them thrive locally and abroad.

'Being a black student at Stellenbosch was pretty difficult. It was almost like being invisible.'

'I loved being involved in the actual farming of the grapes.
My office was the wide expanse of vineyards.'

NTSIKI BIYELA

LIKE CLIMBING TABLE MOUNTAIN

As a young winemaker, you always have to prove yourself. You have to be on top of your game because each and every year you're expressing yourself through your wine. It's never-ending.

If someone had said when I was growing up that I was going to be a winemaker, I wouldn't have thought anything of it. I had no idea what it was, but growing up I knew that I could be anything. My grandmother, despite her financial struggles, made me believe I could do anything I wanted.

I grew up in a village called KwaNondlovu and moved to KwaVuthela in Mahlabatini in KwaZulu-Natal when I was 15 years old. I lived with my grandmother because my mother was working in Durban as a domestic worker. I only saw my mother once a year. Most of the parents of the kids in the village were in the city working, and we all lived with our grandparents.

My daily routine was to wake up, milk the cows, take the cows to the field and then head for school. When I took the cows to the dip where they got treated for ticks, I was the only girl, and when I arrived with my cows, the leader in the village would say, 'She's a girl, let her pass first.' This made the boys so mad.

I also had to fetch wood and go to the river with the other girls to do the washing.

The walk to school took about 30 minutes. In the morning we'd walk very fast because we always left home late. But in the afternoon we dawdled and walked slowly, laughing and talking together. Life felt simple.

When I was in Standard 5 my grandfather died. It was a struggle for my grandmother, especially financially. I don't know how she did it, but she pulled through. She had so many kids to take care of on her tiny pension. She represented love at its best. When she passed away in 2006 I felt like my world had collapsed.

I wasn't aware of apartheid growing up. We were isolated in our little village. I would hear stories that my grandmother would tell about people being arrested when she visited my grandfather in Durban. Other than that, I had no idea of what was happening on the other side.

But in 1994, when all South Africans voted for the first time, I remember that queue. I used to go with my grandmother to queue to collect her pension but on that day it was the longest queue I've ever seen. There were police everywhere. People stood in the sun, patiently, the whole day. Everyone knew it was a life-changing moment for all of us.

I matriculated from Mahlabatini High School in 1996.

I went to Stellenbosch by chance, really. When we were in matric we were given application forms to apply to Stellenbosch to do agriculture. The teacher handing out the forms reminded us that we'd be taught in Afrikaans if we went there. I don't know if anyone else took a form but I asked my Afrikaans teacher, Mr Ngema, to help me fill it in. At the same time I also applied for an SAA Wine Education Bursary.

A month later I got a call from SAA who offered me a full bursary. I cried. They were going to pay for everything. It was a huge break for me, a life-changing moment. It was only afterwards that I realised that I'd applied to do a BSc in viticulture and oenology, and I had no idea what that was! They were giving me a full scholarship to study something and I didn't know what it was! I checked on the internet and realised that it had to do with wine: oenology is winemaking and viticulture is grape-growing.

When an old man from my village heard I was going to be studying wine, he pulled me aside and said, 'My child, out of everything, you went and studied agriculture. Couldn't you just do a secretarial job and be in an office? You're educated. You must be in an office.' Agriculture is something we do here [in the village] all the time. There's nothing glamorous about it.

Some people in the village thought that because I was being sponsored by SAA, I was going to study to be a pilot. When they realised that I was going to study winemaking, they said, 'Oh no: alcohol. That's a problem.' But my grandmother was supportive.

In 1999 I headed off to Stellenbosch University.

Living in Stellenbosch was complicated. Everything was different. I came from rural KwaZulu-Natal where I only saw black people, and Stellenbosch is 99,9% white and Afrikaans-speaking. What made it more difficult was that some students would ask you why you came to an Afrikaans university if you couldn't speak Afrikaans. I felt like punching someone in the face but I couldn't. All I could do was sometimes answer them with anger.

On my first day we got into the hall and sat down, and the lecturer started talking in Afrikaans. I didn't understand a word. When he was done, I saw everyone standing up and leaving, so I realised he must be finished.

In my first year I stayed in Cloetesville, a coloured township outside Stellenbosch, because I was told that accommodation in student residences was full. There were often men standing around where I stayed, making remarks. I felt very uncomfortable there, so I spoke to one of my friends and she said you have to go on campus and ask for accommodation, and if they don't give it to you, just cry.

TOP RIGHT: *Ntsiki outside a store she visited as a child in Mahlabatini.*
CENTRE RIGHT: *Ntsiki with grandmother Sabina, and aunt Thandazile Sibiya.*
BOTTOM LEFT: *Ntsiki and her mother, Margaret Sibiya.*

I went to the administrator and he said there was only accommodation for people who were 18 or 19 years old; I was 20. I just burst into tears and he said, 'Okay, I'll sort something out.' The following day he called me to say there was accommodation and that I was going to stay at Erica [hostel]. So there was always space. Why did I have to cry to get it?

We were only four black students at Erica. It didn't take me long to adjust and I eventually made friends. It was the first time that I had made friends with white people.

I went to lots of formal dances where you had to dress up and do this typical Afrikaans dance called sokkie; they call it langarm. We didn't do that in Mahlabatini. I remember at our final-year party I was dancing with one of my friends, Adriaan, and I told him, 'If there's one thing I've got out of Stellenbosch – I can sokkie!'

I'm still in contact with some of the people in my class. We're in the industry together and we cheer on each other's achievements.

It was tough being taught in Afrikaans but we made a plan. The lecturer would lecture in Afrikaans and I would follow in the English book, looking for similar words. Then I would go back and make my own notes.

I remember my oenology lecturer, Charl Theron. He gave us extra lessons and notes in English to explain difficult concepts. Sometimes he would lecture in English, even if students made a noise and complained.

But I hated physics the most because I failed it several times. I'd done physics in high school and everything looked the same but it was just difficult. In chemistry at school we did experiments but it wasn't in depth because there was no proper equipment or chemicals to use.

I remember thinking, in my first year, *Why do I have to do chemistry and physics? What has it got to do with winemaking?* It was only later when I realised that I needed to understand the reactions of certain chemicals I was using when making wine. Gillian Arendse, our physics lecturer, always went the extra mile to assist us with notes and extra lessons.

In December of my first year, I got a job at Delheim in Stellenbosch, and that's when I fell in love with winemaking. I worked on weekends and during harvest in summertime. On Saturdays, if there were open bottles, they said we could take them, which was so exciting because I was getting good wine for free. I would come back to the hostel and my friends were waiting: 'What did you bring?'

At Delheim I met Philip Costandius, the winemaker. He was so passionate about making wine. I wanted to be a winemaker like him.

There were many times during my studies that I was convinced I would fail. I would call home and cry, 'It's all in Afrikaans and I don't understand anything.' When I checked my results at the end and saw that I'd passed, I felt like I'd climbed Table Mountain and was standing at the top.

When I finished varsity, I was still working at Delheim part-time. I applied to a couple of wineries for a job, with no luck. I remember that there was this one company that said they were looking for a guy. I cried. What is it that a guy can do that I can't?

I called Jabulani Ntshangase and he told me to send my CV to Stellekaya. In my interview, Dave Lello took me to the cellar and I remember thinking, *Please hire me. This cellar is so beautiful.* A few days later they called me to tell me I had the job. That's how I started at Stellekaya, where I worked for 13 years.

Working at Stellekaya was an amazing experience. I learned this vast sweep of knowledge – from the vineyard side to the consumer – which winemakers working in big vineyards don't get.

In the beginning I had difficulties with farmers. I was young and black and they thought, *What does she know about wine?* But as time went on, things changed. I built strong relationships with farmers and we work well together now.

The first award I got was in 2006 – the Michelangelo International Wine Award for my Cape Cross 2004. The function was white and dominated by men. I remember Tariro Masayiti, a winemaker from Zimbabwe who I'd studied with, was there. We were the only two black people, and when they announced that I'd won, the waiters jumped up and down, and I jumped up and danced with them. Then I returned to my table and we all shook hands.

I decided to take my wine that won gold home to my grandmother to taste. I told her it had won a gold medal and she was happy. I poured it into cups and she took a sip. She told me it was nice but her facial expression said the complete opposite. But I could see the pride and excitement in her. As horrible as this tasted, she was really proud her granddaughter had made this.

In 2012, I started my own wine brand, Aslina, named after my grandmother. She helped me keep my feet on the ground. I hope I can be half as strong as her.

In 2017, I had my first harvest of Chardonnay. On the day of the harvest it was exciting to be with Philip, my mentor and teacher from Delheim, from whom I'd bought the grapes. We harvested five tons and Philip told me it was one of his proudest moments too. 'I was there in the beginning when you started as a student,' he said.

'I love this ever-changing content in a bottle. I love that you never know, because everything is nature dependent. You are dealing with new things all the time. Winemaking is like life, everything depends on nature and you nurture that. Some things you have to guide and others you just have to let be.'

FROM VINEYARD TO CELLAR

BEING A WINEMAKER

The job of a winemaker is to take grapes from a vineyard, select the best ones and turn them into the best possible wine through a fermentation and ageing process. It's a journey that starts in the vineyard and ends when you drink and enjoy a glass of wine.

As a winemaker, the season comes but once a year and you have to maximise that opportunity to create the best you can. 'What makes my job interesting,' says winemaker Carmen Stevens, 'is that every year is different. You have a different climatic condition and that influences how those grapes will come out. You then have to decide how you're going to process that specific fruit to get the best out of that vintage.'

'Every winemaker puts his or her own personality into a wine. If people enjoy your wine, they are enjoying you as the person you are,' says Carmen.

GROWING GRAPES

Erna Blancquaert, viticulture lecturer at Stellenbosch University, believes that good wine is made in the vineyard. Every wine has its own personality. That personality comes from the grapes, which have their own character. And that character represents the soil where the grapes were planted, and the season. 'The viticulturist is like the parent of the grape vine,' she says, 'she or he must know their product; how it grows and what it needs to grow well. Viticulture, the science and study of grape cultivation, entails a lot of processes, from selecting the right cultivar for a specific site, to planting the grapes. The viticulturist takes care of the grape, when to plant and what to plant, the elevation and what type of soil preparation is needed. She decides whether or not to irrigate, when to harvest and what type of pruning to apply. All these practises impact on the final quality of the grape. Of course, you also need a winemaker who makes key decisions after the grapes have been picked. But you always need good-quality grapes to start the process off.'

Viticulturist Unathi Mantshongo says she learnt all about viticulture from winemaker Adi Badenhorst. 'He gave me a four-wheeler bike and I rode around the vineyards. I drove around tasting grapes, taking samples and giving him information about when grapes were ready to harvest. I learned when to harvest grapes, how to harvest, how to decide when a vine needs water, or when a vine needs food. I learned about insects, the difference between friendly and dangerous ones. You need to understand how much water you give a vine, how much you stress it so that it produces specific flavours. There is a whole science around growing grapes and making wine, which is fascinating.'

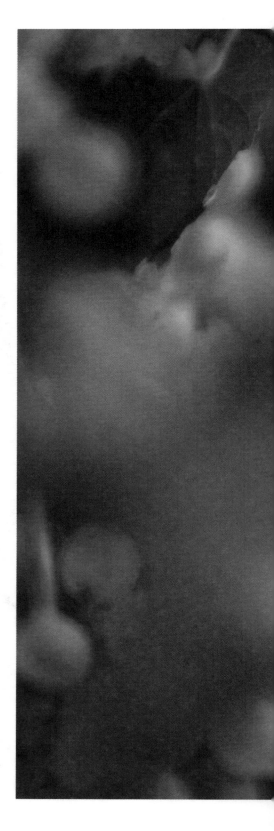

THE HARVEST

Grapes should be picked at optimum ripeness. You don't want to pick them green and you don't want to pick them too ripe either. You want the right character and freshness in the fruit.

Ntsiki Biyela explains: 'If the grapes are too ripe you get a high sugar content, which in turn will give you a high alcohol level in your wine, and you don't want either. You monitor your vineyard by taking regular samples and then estimating when the grapes are ready to harvest. But nature is nature, so you also have to keep a close eye on the weather. When to harvest is usually decided three or four days before picking. You just never know: sometimes the weather changes and you decide to pick today because if you leave it another day it might get too hot.

'Grape pickers work incredibly fast. They know where to hold the bunch so it doesn't break. And where exactly to clip and cut so that they don't damage the vine. They know what to pick and what to leave behind. For example, they leave bunches that are infected with a mealybug. It's important to do that selection in the vineyard because once you've picked the grapes, unless you have a sorting table at the crushing point, the infected grapes will find their way into the bottle.'

IN THE CELLAR: FROM BARRELS TO BOTTLES

After the grapes have been picked, they go to the wine cellar to be crushed and put into tanks. Gerry Algernon (top left, opposite) is the cellar supervisor at Summerhill Wines in Stellenbosch. He explains, 'I make sure that the press is running smoothly and the crates of grapes keep moving into the press. When the grapes arrive, I make sure they're crushed and that the tanks are clean. I add the chemicals that the winemaker asks for, like sulphur and enzymes.'

After the grapes are pressed, the juice goes into tanks where the winemaker adds enzymes so that it can settle before going to the barrels. In the barrels, nutrients and yeast are added. Ntsiki explains: 'Wine is like a person. It needs to eat right. You feed the yeast, so it will ferment and sugars are converted into alcohol. The winemaker continues to taste in order to monitor the balance of the wine and assess when it is ready. Once ready, the wine is moved from the barrels into bottles, where it stays for a while. Reds take eight months to three years, and whites take six months to a year, to settle in the bottle.'

When wine is maturing in the barrels, you start doing the blending. You take the personalities of the different cultivars and put them together, to achieve something different but harmonious. It's like cooking. The quality of the dish depends on how you blend the different ingredients. For Carmen, the art of winemaking is in the blending. 'I love to blend. I love to experiment. You taste through to the final product and decide how to blend up this wine, to bring out the best of that vintage.'

FOR THE LOVE OF WINE

'A senior colleague of mine once advised that if I didn't drink red wine, I wouldn't have the sophistication I needed to succeed in business. So I slowly started drinking red wine till I got used to it. Now it's my drink of choice.'
— *Manana Nhlanhla, director, Kalipha Foundation*

'The first time I drank wine was when I'd finished high school and went to university. We were sitting around debating South African politics because the country was undergoing big changes. We drank cheap wine. What I like about wine is that it makes people relax, and you can sit around and have a conversation.'
— *Professor Sean Jacobs, The New School, New York*

'I grew up in Chatsworth in Durban, into a large extended family. No one in the family drank alcohol; it wasn't around at all. After I finished my degree I became curious to try wine and have enjoyed exploring different wines ever since. I especially love discovering new wines when I travel; you get to taste a country, its soil and people. I have tasted Malbec in Argentina, Bordeaux blends in France and delicious Merlots in Turkey. Wine is about friendship and discovery. With every bottle, you figure out your taste anew.'
— *Mervyn Shanmugam, CEO, Sanlam Alternative Investments*

'I like the taste of wine. I like the smell of wine. I like opening a bottle of wine and the excitement of what you're going to get. My favourite is wine in summer. I love a really nice white wine with a beautiful sunset: the combination of wine, food and a beautiful background.'
— *Unathi Mantshongo, viticulturist*

THE WORLD
OF WINE

A SHORT HISTORY OF WINE IN SOUTH AFRICA

Michelle Hay

'There are two narratives about the history of winemaking in South Africa. The first tells of a patchwork of exquisite wine farms stretching across the southern slopes of Table Mountain and pristine vineyards waiting to be harvested. The other tells the story of an industry built on the back of slaves, restricted and constrained by apartheid regulation and dominated by a small elite and wealthy white minority.' — Danie du Toit, historian

San hunter-gatherer communities lived in the Cape for tens of thousands of years, and Khoekhoen herders resided there for many centuries, prior to the arrival of the first white settlers.[1] In 1652 the Dutch East India Company (Vereenigde Oostindische Compagnie, or VOC) established a station at the Cape to provide for its ships rounding the tip of Africa. After building a fort, the VOC began producing some of its own goods to reduce the costs of running the station and earn more income. They encouraged employees to grow vegetables in their gardens, with the help of slaves brought with them to the Cape. Soon, they began thinking about wheat and wine.

THE FIRST LAND GRAB

The first land grants were made to nine men discharged from the service of the VOC, and marked the beginning of a long history of land dispossession in the Cape. The land was in the Liesbeek River valley, a relatively sheltered area suitable for growing wheat, and where local Khoekhoen grazed their livestock.

Unhappy about the incursion of the VOC settlement, among other things, the Khoekhoen organised themselves under Doman, 'a man of common origin but uncommon skill', who'd been an interpreter for the Dutch and knew their intentions.[2] They attacked in 1659. The Khoekhoen were defeated, and this pattern would be repeated over the course of the next 50 years as more land was granted to settlers in what is today known as the Cape Winelands. The Khoekhoen were subject to violent livestock raids by settlers and, in later years, from slaves who had escaped captivity.

Jan van Riebeeck recorded in a report back to Holland in 1660: 'The reasons advanced by them for … making war upon us last year, arising out of complaints that our people, living at a distance, and without our knowledge … had done them much injury and also perhaps stolen and eaten up some of their sheep and calves etc. in which there is also some truth and which it is very hard to keep the common people from doing, when a little out of sight; so they think they had cause for revenge, and especially, they said, upon people who had come to take and to occupy the land which had been their own in all ages, turning with the plough and cultivating permanently their best land, and keeping them off the ground upon which they had been accustomed to depasture their cattle, so they must consequently now seek their subsistence by depasturing the land of other people, from which nothing could arise but disputes with their neighbours; insisting so strenuously upon the point of restoring to them their own land, that we were at length compelled to say they had entirely forfeited that right, through the war which they had waged against us, and that we were not inclined to restore it, as it now had become the property of the Company by the sword and the laws of war.'[3]

Another insidious effect of this culture clash was a growing dependency on alcohol, as the Dutch bartered brandy (among other luxuries) with the Khoekhoen for their cattle, which the herders found hard to resist. Through theft and barter, the Khoekhoen slowly lost the basis of their wealth. Destitute and landless, many became labourers on the future wine and wheat farms.

THE FIRST WINES

The first wines produced by Cape farmers were infamously bad, with some flavoured by the pigskin bags they were kept in, previously used to store pickles.[4] Winemaking technology was rudimentary, manufacturing techniques crude and standards low. But with the VOC and passing ships providing a guaranteed market, and their competitors far away in Europe, there was little need for improvement.

The quality of wine did improve, however, with the arrival of Simon van der Stel in 1679. He was a wine enthusiast who introduced new techniques and established new estates after granting himself prime land in Constantia.

As an employee of the VOC as well as Governor of the Cape, Van der Stel passed regulations that ensured the VOC got all of the produce it needed, and which inhibited the wine industry. He declared, for example, that 'every person who shall plant a morgen of vines shall be bound to cultivate six morgen of other crops'.[5]

In the meantime, he spent a lot of energy on his own wine estate. Eventually, under the custodianship of the Cloete family, who took over after Van der Stel's death, the estate produced the finest fortified wine of the Cape. Constantia wine was sought after by European royalty. Napoléon Bonaparte himself, on his deathbed in exile on St Helena, is said to have refused everything offered to him but a glass of Constantia wine.

FRENCH IMMIGRANTS ARRIVE

Winemaking improved further from 1685 when Protestants fleeing persecution in France arrived in the Cape, bringing with them winemaking skills and more refined tastes than those of the local garrison. While slightly better than before, however, the quality of wine in general remained poor.

The Huguenots, as the French immigrants became known, settled mainly in Stellenbosch, Franschhoek and Wellington. They lived interspersed with Dutch farmers, and over time these mixed 'free burghers' would identify as Afrikaners, making the Cape their permanent home and distinguishing themselves from company employees who expected to return to Europe.

One of the biggest problems facing the growing industry was overproduction. The market for South African wine was small, and from around 1699 it became dominated by senior employees of the VOC, including Van der Stel and his sons. With large estates and the use of the VOC's slaves, they used their privileged access to the VOC to monopolise the trade in wine and meat to such an extent that the livelihoods of free burghers came under threat. Further white settlement was deemed unnecessary, because there was no need for more farmers, and prospective white immigrants were turned away.

The free burghers protested, and a change of leadership in the VOC saw Simon van der Stel removed from his post. As a result, from the early eighteenth century the colony expanded at a faster rate, as more immigrants arrived from Europe. This put further pressures on the Khoekhoen, but encouraged the growth of the wine industry.

EARLY SLAVES

The early wine industry, like the colony itself, relied on slaves and the semi-enslaved Khoekhoen for labour.

The first slaves in the colony arrived with the first white settlers in 1652. To acquire more slaves, the VOC launched expeditions, first to Dahomey, then to Mozambique, the east coast of Africa and Madagascar. These slaves were for the company's own use and made up a minority of slaves in the country. Most slaves – about 58 500 between 1652 and 1808 – entered the colony through the private trade;[6] they came from Madagascar, India, the Indonesian archipelago, and a few came from the east African coast and Mauritius. They suffered inhuman conditions on the ships they travelled in, with no sanitation, natural light or food under the decks, in conditions so overcrowded there was no space to turn.

Khoekhoen labourers provided seasonal labour at harvest time, joining the slaves on the local wheat farms from December to February, and the wine farms in March. Slaves and Khoekhoen had despised each other in the early years of the Cape Colony but once they started to live and work together on farms they became allies. Some slave men and Khoekhoen women became partners and had children.

THE 'DOP' OR TOT SYSTEM AND LABOUR TENANCY

One of the most notorious labour practises was the 'dop' or tot system, in which labourers were 'paid' with servings of cheap white wine. A man named Job, a slave on a farm in Graaff-Reinet, recalled: 'The day began shortly after dawn … At 11 o'clock, the slaves ate their first meal, a thick soup of peas, beans and Indian corn or barley. Occasionally there was meat with their soup. Always there was wine to drink. The slaves received a half a pint in the morning and evening, and in summer a third half-pint at midday. After eating, the slaves rested, smoking or sleeping for perhaps an hour and a half before returning to work. In the evening, there was more soup, again with a tot of wine.'[7]

In the nineteenth century, the Cape was ceded to Great Britain. The dop system, used to justify low wages because part of the 'wage' was in alcohol, was prohibited by the British in 1809. It continued, however, and created a large-scale dependency of farm workers on alcohol and the people who supplied it.

Slavery was abolished in 1833, but farmers attracted and/or controlled labourers in other ways. It was usual, for example, to give workers some land on which they could grow crops in exchange for labour. This was the system of labour tenancy, which made tenants vulnerable to eviction if they ever disobeyed a farmer. But it was also resented by farmers because it meant giving workers some independent means of production.

While the wine industry struggled with labour issues, the British recognised that it had potential. The number of vines planted more than doubled in 17 years, from 15 million in 1808 to 32 million in 1825.[8] Wine became the Cape's most important export commodity, making up 90% of exports between 1810 and the 1820s.[9] The Cape's biggest market was Britain, thanks to imperial preference policies that meant that wines from the Cape could be sold much cheaper than that of their competitors. The low cost of South African wine was important for the industry because, with a few exceptions, the quality of the wines was still relatively poor.

When the imperial preference policy was abolished in 1825, exports to Britain dropped by 75% and despite a brief rally in the mid-1800s, the industry continued to decline in the second half of the century.[10] There were also crop diseases, including infestation of phylloxera, an insect pest that ravaged grape vines.

Despite the challenging international market and undeveloped local market, farmers continued growing vines and making poor-quality wine, and overproduction continued to plague the industry. Faced with these challenges, wine farmers began to get organised in order to defend their economic interests.

KWV TAKES CONTROL

The Koöperatieve Wijnbouwers Vereniging van Zuid-Afrika (KWV) was established in 1916 as a cooperative. It aimed to regulate the price of wine produced by its members and to promote the sale of their products. By the end of the following year, about 90% of wine farmers in the Cape had become members. The exceptions were the wine farmers from Constantia, and a few from Stellenbosch, who were producing good wine that they had no trouble marketing, and which fetched a higher price on an open market than the KWV would pay them.

The KWV was formally registered in 1918. Essentially, it was a way of dealing with the problems of overproduction and marketing: rather than asking wine farmers to limit production (which would stabilise the price of wine) or improve the quality of the wine (which might make it more marketable overseas), the KWV bought produce at a set price and in this way simply made any surplus 'disappear'. There was relatively little interest in good-quality wine because most wine went to the production of average brandy.

Merchants and distillers were opposed to this, because they had to buy wine through the KWV at a much higher price than if they'd bought directly from farmers. Their opposition led to its near collapse, but the National Party and the government, who were supportive of the KWV, passed a string of legislation that gave the KWV special powers, such as control over wine for distilling (making fortified wines and brandy). Other merchants and manufacturers had to buy distilling wine from the KWV at an elevated price and so could not possibly compete.

The Wine and Spirits Control Amendment Act of 1940 further extended the KWV's control and gave them powers to limit production. Additional laws passed during the apartheid years included the infamous Wine and Spirits Control Act of 1970 (the 'KWV Act'), which ensured that the KWV maintained its monopoly and rose above any competition. Eventually, the KWV could set production quotas, limit the size of production, and set floor prices. It inserted itself into different levels of the wine industry, from buying grapes to manufacturing, and distributing and selling wine – normally things done by different companies. The KWV effectively controlled the wine industry and supported the enrichment of a small, politically connected white elite.

WINE AND WORKERS IN THE TWENTIETH CENTURY

While the government protected the KWV and a small group of elite wine farmers, it did not protect the labourers and tenants who worked in the wine industry. The KWV failed to eradicate the dop system, and in fact, in the 1920s, wanted to extend the dop

system to the then South African provinces of Transvaal and Natal. Labourers on wine farms continued to be slaves to alcohol.

Other industries, such as the mining industry, also used alcohol to lure people into the cash economy, eventually compelling them to work for low wages. As wine-industry veteran Michael Fridjhon puts it, 'Alcohol has been an instrument of repression in the history of apartheid South Africa. We can't wish that away.'[11]

In the twentieth century farmers were the 'masters', with enormous power over labourers. They had to feed labourers and house them, but wages were low and the dop system prevailed. Labourers were also very tightly controlled when it came to their movements and ability to represent themselves. While some farmers were humane, the system allowed for extensive abuse.

The increase in demand for urban labour in the 1960s led to a shortage of farm labour. This was a familiar problem around the country and led to the use of black prisoners, often imprisoned for pass-law offences, as farm labour. It also led to policies to improve conditions for coloured rural communities, and to subsidise farm housing.[12]

APARTHEID

From the 1970s, and particularly in the 1980s, the apartheid government faced increasing scrutiny for its human-rights abuses, and eventually sanctions from the international community.

South Africa's system of racial segregation and apartheid was reaching new heights of social control over blacks and the denial of their rights. The government accelerated its programme of forced removals of Africans from their land, introduced new policies that would condemn black children to a poor-quality education, and used increasingly violent means to suppress political activists fighting for freedom and equality.

While many were forced into exile to escape imprisonment, torture or death, thousands of others engaged in violent protests, such as the Soweto school riots in 1976. The tempo of resistance and suppression increased. But even heavy censorship couldn't prevent the world from witnessing the apartheid government's abuses. 'The world refused to drink South African wine. They could taste in it the bitterness of apartheid,' notes writer Tim James.[13]

At the same time, globalisation – the free movement of goods, services and people across the world – became a major force, compelling countries to end protectionist policies or face exclusion from international markets. Facing international scrutiny, the wine industry, along with the country as a whole, tried to sanitise its image. This opened up a space for progressives to try to bring about change in the wine sector too.

The Rural Foundation was set up in the 1980s to improve the social conditions of workers in the Western Cape farming community, although its influence later spread to other parts of the country. The Foundation encouraged greater community engagement; and its members paid workers higher wages, and introduced things like community halls, TV rooms and crèches. But the structures of power remained the same, with whites as bosses and blacks as workers.[14]

Nevertheless, the Rural Foundation pioneered efforts to reform the wine industry, and improve the lives and prospects of farm workers at a time when the industry was extremely conservative. Its members braved ostracism and aggression to push the agenda for change. They set an example that progressive farmers continue to follow today, although the Rural Foundation no longer exists.

Changes to the industry began in the 1980s and early 1990s as the international environment became more hostile to South Africa. But it was only in 1994, with the first democratic election, when millions of black South Africans could vote for the first time, that real change could begin to take place.

On 27 April 1994, standing all day in baking heat and snaking queues, all South Africans, black and white, made their marks at polling booths across the country. The African National Congress (ANC) was voted into power. South Africa had finally succeeded in throwing off the shackles of apartheid and becoming a democracy. Nelson Mandela became president, and with a carefully appointed cabinet began the enormous challenge of transforming the country.

It was an event that allowed the re-entry of Cape wine into world markets. John Platter called 1994 'a lifeboat and a new dawn for Cape wine'.[15]

'Alcohol has been an instrument of repression in the history of apartheid South Africa. We can't wish that away.'
— Michael Fridjhon

'The world refused to drink South African wine. They could taste in it the bitterness of apartheid.' — Tim James

POST-APARTHEID:
THE CHALLENGE OF CHANGE

But what was South Africa to transform into? After years of damaging sanctions, the country had an opportunity to re-enter the international community. Furthermore, the era of globalisation had begun, and, as Bongiwe Njobe, the director-general of the South African Department of Agriculture between 1997 and 2004, put it, 'If you wanted to participate in global markets, you couldn't have a controlled trading environment in your own country.'[16]

The ANC was also expected to deliver on its promises of improving the lives of black people by ensuring that political and economic power would be shared; that labour, which was predominantly black, would be better protected; and that land reform would take place.

Deregulation – essentially, dismantling the structures that had propped up apartheid – took place in a context of profound changes throughout the country. Derek Hanekom, a farmer and member of the ANC who'd spent years in jail as a political prisoner, became the new Minister of Agriculture and Land Affairs. Like many development economists at the time, he believed in the transformative power of free markets, and he took a speedy track to deregulate the agricultural sector as a whole. Most people believe that deregulation created new opportunities and was a lifeboat for the industry.

Sithembiso Mthethwa, director of the Kalipha Foundation, recalls, 'When sanctions were lifted, it suddenly meant that South Africa was open for business. It created opportunity for those who were ready. Opportunity is ready to dance with those who're on the dance floor. It spawned a whole new sector of activity and raised the bar. But the downside of being in a cocooned environment for so long is that you're exposed to only what you have in front of you. So it was exciting and daunting at the same time.'[17]

Hanekom instituted reforms that affected the KWV and its monopoly of power. In Hanekom's own words, 'KWV in 1996 decided that it wanted to become a listed company. At that time it was a cooperative with statutory powers. Some wine farmers objected to this and brought to my attention as minister that they [KWV] were now becoming a company competing on the open market, but with huge and unfair advantages over other companies because of assets that they had accumulated and acquired as a result of their statutory powers under apartheid. They had accumulated approximately R1,8 billion-worth of assets and as far as we were concerned they had to make this money available to the industry.'[18]

The KWV was taken to court, and there was a settlement and agreement that R369 million-worth of assets would be placed in a trust to put back into the industry to support transformation. But some people were disappointed with the performance of the Wine Industry Trust. According to Bongiwe Njobe: 'Regrettably, the Trust was not really effective in steering transformation because it didn't act as a lever for change. In hindsight, maybe we should have said that the only thing the fund would support was training and to offset the cost of capital to enter the industry.'[19]

Derek Hanekom's successor, Thoko Didiza, arranged an empowerment deal with the KWV that ultimately meant that the KWV didn't have to pay the government the money it owed but gave out shares instead. Meanwhile, the rest of the money accumulated through years of controlling the industry – funds which should have been public – was kept by established white farmers.

The response to efforts at transformation had been mixed. Some argue that the KWV and established white farmers were left with too many of the assets built up over the years of controlling the industry. Others point out that while the amounts transferred may have been inadequate, some successes were achieved.

JOINING GLOBAL MARKETS

Entering the global market offered new opportunities and challenges for the wine industry, even though years of control had meant that 'farmers were not incentivised to produce the most or the best. They were incentivised to produce the product that earned them the best possible subsidy,' as Fridjhon notes.[20] Wine farmers were 'not up there' in terms of the quality the global market expected.

Competing on a global scale, entering new markets, and with an entirely new, positive image, the wine industry could finally rebrand itself. However, initially, this wasn't done very well. 'After sanctions were dropped and South Africa was allowed back into the international arena, we didn't think properly how to pitch ourselves,' says Thandi Wines managing director Vernon Henn. 'A door had opened and everyone ran through to sell more wine. I think we positioned ourselves quite badly by going for the cheaper stuff to get volume. That created the perception in the international community that South African wine was cheap wine – cheap and cheerful.'[21]

Platter pointed out nevertheless that opening world markets for the industry was 'the saving grace' for South African wines and the beginning of a 'fantastic revolution in quality'.[22]

The quantity and quality of South African wine did increase dramatically. Wine exports increased from 25 million litres in 1993 to well over 400 million litres per year since 2012.[23] South Africa exports roughly 50% of its wine, which has kept the industry viable. As Hanekom says, 'Two decades ago there were one or two good-quality export wines. Today there are dozens and dozens of excellent-quality export wines.'[24]

POOR LABOUR CONDITIONS

Sadly, however, while there has been a revolution in the quality of South African wines, labour conditions on many farms remain poor. While conditions have undoubtedly improved on some farms, on others, workers still struggle for basic things like a living wage, electricity or protective equipment when using toxic pesticides.[25]

The impetus to improve wages and living conditions on farms has come not only from government policies but also from UK supermarkets that import South African wine. They demand that their suppliers ascribe to fair-trade principles, which include good working conditions. The Wine and Agricultural Ethical Trade Association (WIETA) was formed in 2002 as a not-for-profit voluntary organisation to monitor on-farm labour standards.

However, deprived of government support since 1994, and thrust into a competitive global market, wine farmers have struggled to manage additional labour costs. The global

Nelson and Winnie Mandela on the day of Madiba's release from Victor Verster Prison, Paarl, 11 February 1990.

recession caused by the financial crisis of 2008, and periodic droughts, have added to farmers' financial woes.

Unable and sometimes unwilling to improve conditions for all workers, the wine industry has seen increasing casualisation of labour.[26] The result is that only about a third of people working in the wine industry are permanent workers who live in and around wine farms. The rest are seasonal workers, finding temporary jobs during harvest time, moving from place to place depending on the season, but most often struggling to find work and living in desperate conditions.

Black African workers struggle more than coloured workers, because they're seen as being more militant and unionised. They also don't have the same networks and family connections that help many coloureds get jobs on the wine farms.[27] In this context, workers are often scared of joining unions. Only about 3% of workers in the Western Cape agricultural sector are unionised, compared to 30% in the country as a whole.[28]

THE 2012 WORKERS' STRIKE

Seasonal workers went on strike in 2012, demanding better wages and conditions. The strikes seemed to be spontaneous, arising out of local grievances, and soon became violent.

Although striking workers weren't unionised, trade unions such as the Black Association for the Wine and Spirit Industry (BAWSI), the BAWSI Agricultural Workers' Union of South Africa (BAWUSI) and the Congress of South African Trade Unions (Cosatu) became involved. They attempted to reach a settlement through dialogue between striking farm workers, business and government.

With pressure from striking workers, the minimum wage was raised from R69 to R105 a day – an improvement, but far off the R150-a-day workers wanted, and a wage that would still leave them among the poorest in the country.

While some are hopeful about increasing dialogue and farm worker organisation since the strike, actual conditions have generally not improved. For example, in 2017 a WIETA audit found that Groot Constantia, a formerly state-owned farm, was in breach of its ethical guidelines and various laws.[29] They were storing dangerous chemicals unsafely, providing contaminated drinking water to workers, failing to protect workers from toxic substances, failing to provide contracts to others, and keeping others on casual contracts long after they should have been provided with better job security. Evictions still take place, and housing is in poor condition, with access to it tightly controlled.

In an interview with the *Mail & Guardian*, Zann Maho, who has worked at Groot Constantia for nine years, said she was 'confused and angry' about how a not-for-profit company, which she thought should be 'investing in the lives of workers', could allow her family to live in a house in such a bad condition that the roof was in danger of collapsing.[30]

LAND REFORM

OPPOSITE: *Farm worker strikes in 2012 across the Western Cape.*

Another programme introduced to transform agriculture was land reform, intended to return land to black people who were dispossessed due to racist land policies, and bring about rural development. Land reform was also meant to tackle gender inequality, giving women a greater stake in the land.

But the impact of land reform in the country as a whole has been poor. Thousands of land claims have still not been settled. There are also questions around the extent to which land has actually been transferred to beneficiaries to alleviate poverty. This slow pace of reform is due to a number of factors, including lack of support, skills, financing and corruption.

Land reform in the wine sector hasn't extensively changed the racial profile of land ownership, although it has given many black people access to land through other schemes. But by accessing land predominantly through trusts and community-based organisations, land-reform beneficiaries often miss out on the benefits of private land ownership, such as making independent decisions on how to use land, and whether to sell. They're also often burdened with the disadvantages of community ownership, such as complex decision-making processes and internal disputes.

Land reform in the Western Cape has also exacerbated tensions between African, coloured and 'Khoi Nation' claimants. Khoi Nation groups in particular feel they are missing out on land reform. The claimants identify as the descendants of the Khoekhoen groups brutally dispossessed in the seventeenth century, and whose subsequent exploitation underpinned the growth of the wine industry. They have lodged claims for the return of this land, which includes the Cape Winelands. However, the land-restitution programme was not designed with these kinds of claims in mind: restitution deals only with dispossession that occurred after 1913 as a result of racially discriminatory laws, rather than conquest.

Anger at being excluded from land restitution has been sharpened by the perception that economic-development initiatives and black economic empowerment are aimed at black Africans rather than at the coloured descendants of Khoekhoen/Khoisan groups.

NEW OPPORTUNITIES

Some of the most pressing challenges facing the government and the private sector are to improve working conditions on wine farms and promote greater inclusion of those who currently feel left behind. But despite these challenges, the face of the wine industry *is* changing.

New brands have been created by entrants to the wine industry, and the domestic market for good wine is growing. Black winemakers, viticulturists, sommeliers and other industry players have invigorated South African wine.

New opportunities exist for black individuals to make their mark, and for white farmers, industry players and businesses to show their commitment to transformation. They have had to do so in a difficult environment, and will continue to face challenges. Their unique backgrounds, vision and perseverance will help shape the future of wine in South Africa.

NOTES

1   Two thousand years ago San hunter-gatherers acquired domestic livestock in what is now Botswana. Their population grew and spread throughout the western half of South Africa. They were the first pastoralists in southern Africa, and called themselves Khoikhoi (or Khoekhoen), which means 'men of men' or 'the real people'. They were the first native people to come into contact with the Dutch settlers in the mid-seventeenth century. The settlers used the term 'Bushmen' for the San. Hunters (San) and herders (Khoekhoen) are sometimes lumped together as 'Khoisan'.

2   Elphick, R (1980): 'The Khoisan to 1770' in Elphick, R and Giliomee, H: The Shaping of South African Society, 1652–1840, Cape Town: Longman.

3   Quoted in Wilson, M and Thompson, L (1982): A History of South Africa to 1870, Cape Town: David Philip, p. 65.

4   Fridjhon, M (1986): Conspiracy of Giants: The South African Liquor Industry, Johannesburg: D Stein Publishers.

5   Ibid.

6   Ross, R (2012): 'Khoesan and Immigrants: The Emergence of Colonial Society in the Cape, 1500–1800' in Hamilton, C, Mbenga, BK and Ross, R: The Cambridge History of South Africa, Vol 1, Cambridge: Cambridge University Press.

7   Quoted in Williams, G (2016): 'Slaves, Workers, and Wine: The "Dop" System' in the History of the Cape Wine Industry, 1658–1894', Journal of Southern African Studies, 42 (5), p. 902.

8   Vink, N, Williams, G and Kirsten J (2004): 'South Africa' in Anderson, K: The World's Wine Markets: Globalization at Work, Cheltenham: Edward Elgar Publishing.

9   Ibid.

10   Ibid.

11   Michael Fridjhon interview: The Colour of Wine documentary, 2018.

12   Vink et al. 2004.

13   James, T (2013): Wines of the New South Africa: Tradition and Revolution, Berkeley: University of California Press.

14   Ewert, J and Du Toit, A (2005): 'A Deepening Divide in the Countryside: Restructuring and Rural Livelihoods in the South African Wine Industry', Journal of Southern African Studies, 31 (2), p. 319.

15   John Platter interview: The Colour of Wine documentary, 2018.

16   Bongiwe Njobe interview: The Colour of Wine documentary, 2018.

17   Sithembiso Mthethwa interview: The Colour of Wine documentary, 2018.

18   Derek Hanekom interview: The Colour of Wine documentary, 2018.

19   Bongiwe Njobe interview: The Colour of Wine documentary, 2018.

20   Michael Fridjhon interview: The Colour of Wine documentary, 2018.

21   Vernon Henn interview: The Colour of Wine documentary, 2018.

22   John Platter interview: The Colour of Wine documentary, 2018.

23   Wines of South Africa (2012): 'South African Wine Industry Statistics' https://www.wosa.co.za/The-Industry/Statistics/SA-Wine-Industry-Statistics/ (accessed 23 May 2018).

24   Derek Hanekom interview: The Colour of Wine documentary, 2018.

25   Human Rights Watch (2011): 'South Africa: Farmworkers' Dismal, Dangerous Lives' https://www.hrw.org/news/2011/08/23/south-africa-farmworkers-dismal-dangerous-lives (accessed 23 May 2018).

26   Ewert et al. 2005, pp. 326–328.

27   Ibid.

28   Human Rights Watch 2011.

29   Webster, D (16 March 2018): 'Constantia Leaves Bitter Aftertaste' Mail & Guardian https://mg.co.za/article/2018-03-16-00-constantia-leaves-bitter-aftertaste (accessed 31 May 2018).

30   Ibid.

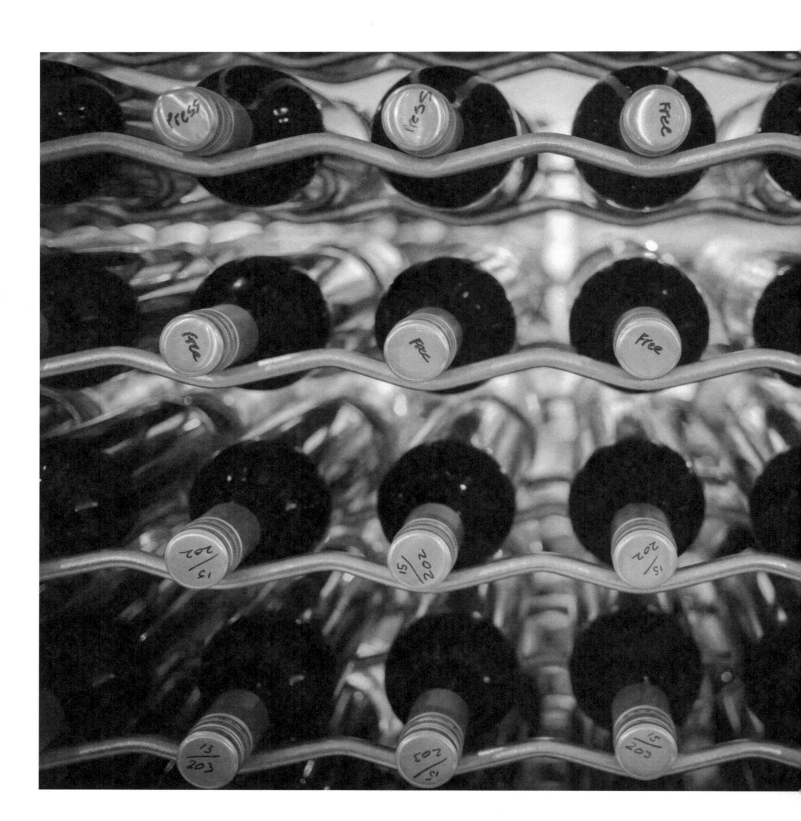

EDUCATION AND CAREER OPPORTUNITIES

WESLEY THOMPSON

'Many of the challenges with training are that we experience a significant deficit in peoples' schooling. Many children are still deprived of decent primary and secondary education. People are at a disadvantage not only in their ability to use information but also in how to apply it.'
— Phil Bowes, transformation and development manager, VinPro

The South African wine industry could generate roughly 100 000 new jobs by 2025,[1] but for many young people, especially black matriculants, working in the wine industry is not their first career choice. On average, 20 black students graduate with a BSc in agriculture from Stellenbosch University every year, compared with 140 white students.[2] The Department of Viticulture and Oenology (DVO) at Stellenbosch University is the only university-based department in South Africa where students can study winemaking. The DVO has become more proactive in driving recruitment and hosts school students, who visit the faculty during school holidays. It also conducts post-matric programmes to improve performance in maths and physical science.

'Winemaking isn't attracting black students because a lot of people don't know about it,' says viticulturist Unathi Mantshongo. Compounding the problem, Unathi adds, is stigma. 'My mother didn't tell people that I was studying winemaking because she obviously could never have allowed her child to go and study liquor-making for four years.'

Erna Blancquaert, lecturer in viticulture at Stellenbosch University, thinks a more obvious reason is a negative perception of agriculture among youth generally today, who seek jobs they perceive to be more glamorous and well-paying in the city. 'I think agriculture as a whole is seen as a no-go. It's perceived as a "dirty" profession where you have to work long hours in the hot sun. Few people understand that agriculture is, in fact, a science.'

Erna, the first black woman in South Africa to get a PhD in viticulture, was exposed to winemaking through her father, who worked at Nederburg. 'He had to drive wine samples to the respective cellars, and I'd go with him, and I was always fascinated by this entire process. Being surrounded by vineyards and seeing vines, I just had to know more. That's what drove me to go and study viticulture and oenology.'

But winemaking isn't a familiar profession to most prospective black students, particularly those who don't live in the Cape winemaking regions and have little exposure to the wine industry. Winemaker Dumisani Mathonsi chose to study winemaking for purely financial reasons – he received a comprehensive bursary that he 'grabbed with both hands' despite having little knowledge of what he was getting into. 'I knew nothing about winemaking, absolutely nothing,' he recalls. 'My family didn't know I was going to study winemaking. I remember coming home and taking some soil samples in the garden. My mother asked me what I was doing. I said I had to take the soil samples back to the university to analyse. She thought it was a joke.'

Erna confirms that many students, like Dumisani, come to Stellenbosch University simply because they have bursaries to study winemaking, and they don't really know what they're signing up for. 'They just enrol or apply for a bursary because there's no other way. Their parents don't earn enough money to send them to any university of their choice so they have to take whatever is available, and they start hating it because it's a culture shock to come to Stellenbosch.'

However, wine writer Michael Fridjhon points out that bursaries have been instrumental in bringing black students into the industry. The SAA Wine Education Bursary Fund, for example, played an important role in the early democratic era. Michael, who was instrumental in setting the Fund up, recalls, 'It made university education in the wine-trading sector available to South Africans who'd never had an opportunity of even contemplating that kind of job. It facilitated the entry of black people into the wine industry.'

The Fund was established in 1994, and in its first year it couldn't find black applicants. Jabulani Ntshangase, a trustee on the Fund who'd recently returned to South Africa after 15 years in exile, went out and literally rounded applicants up. 'The first thing I did,' Jabulani says, 'was go to high schools in KwaZulu-Natal, where I grew up, recruiting youngsters, telling them that there was a career for them out there that their parents, teachers and school principals hadn't heard of.'

Jabulani did more than just recruit the students – he played a key role in supporting and mentoring them through their university years. 'There was no welcoming committee for the students and it was a tough environment. But there were other families and local winemakers who really helped and supported them too.'

Today, there are many bursaries available to black students wanting to study viticulture and oenology at Stellenbosch University. However, the decline in maths and science results at school level is a major impediment. To study winemaking at Stellenbosch, Grade 12 applicants need a minimum pass of 60% in maths and 50% in science. In 2017, of 265 810 matrics who sat for the National Senior Certificate maths exam, 51,5% passed, but the average mark was 30,8%, far below the requirement to

'*Winemaking isn't a familiar profession to most prospective black students.*'

study viticulture and oenology.[3] In matric science, 62% of 192 618 learners passed, with an average mark of 35%, also well short of the threshold to enter winemaking studies.[4] Furthermore, the results of the 2011 Trends in International Mathematics and Science Study (TIMSS), which tests learners' abilities at Grade 8 level, are troubling: South Africa performed the worst of 21 middle-income countries.[5]

Applying maths and science knowledge in practical situations is also a challenge. Dr Gillian Arendse, former physics lecturer at Stellenbosch University, says that this problem has its roots in how learners are educated at school level. 'Even when I was at school, you did experiments out of a textbook,' he recalls, 'and if you ended up mixing chemicals and it didn't quite work out, the teacher would say, "Well, the textbook says it's supposed to be blue, even though it's green, so let's just pretend it's blue." Many learners come out of school with flying colours, but when they get into a tertiary environment the wheels come off, because when you get into higher education, it's not about what you know, it's about what you can do.'

FINDING WORK

Those students who make it through their studies face another challenge – being employable. They often lack the ability to apply their theoretical knowledge in the industry. To ease this transition, various mentoring programmes have been set up, such as the Nedbank Cape Winemakers' Guild (CWG) Protégé Programme established by winemaker Philip Costandius. The programme identifies students of exceptional ability and helps them to become more employable. During a three-year internship, previously disadvantaged graduates are mentored by one of 49 members of the CWG, all winemakers recognised for their excellence and innovation. To date, the programme has produced 24 protégés, and so far, according to Philip, most of the graduates of the programme have been employed.

The Pinotage Youth Development Academy (PYDA), of which Ntsiki Biyela is a board member, is another programme aimed at bridging the gap between studies and

LEFT TO RIGHT:

Dr Erna Blancquaert,
Jabulani Ntshangase,
Philip Costandius,
Dr Gillian Arendse.

the world of work for young black people in the industry. 'Through the PYDA's one-year programme, students are equipped with technical skills in winemaking and viticulture as well as in sales, marketing, tourism and hospitality,' Ntsiki explains. To date, 123 previously disadvantaged students have successfully completed the programme, and 90% of them have found employment within six months of graduating.

The VinPro Foundation offers bursaries for historically disadvantaged graduates to study wine business management, which Unathi says has been very successful. 'We envision building leaders in the wine industry throughout the value chain – so everyone, from the person who's done a science degree, right up to the guy who was a manager at a hotel and did a sommelier course, can do the course. We're trying to transform the leadership of the wine industry.'

There are several vocational-training courses for students who don't qualify to study at university. Every year, the Cape Wine Academy (CWA) provides training to more than 4 500 students, 50% of whom come from tertiary institutions, and 10% of whom are employed in the wine- and food-retail industries.

The CWA's courses range from the basic-level South African Wine Course, which provides an introduction to wines, to the advanced-level Cape Wine Master's programme, the highest formal qualification in the South African wine industry. Since the institution of the Cape Wine Master's programme 33 years ago, 100 graduates have gone on to be committed and knowledgeable advocates for wines, lecturing at the CWA or hosting wine tastings in their communities.

Skills development also needs to happen from the ground up. In 2013, unskilled labour comprised 56% of the wine industry's workforce.[6]

Charl Theron, a wine educator and trainer, says that training is about creating opportunities for workers to grow and develop in their jobs. 'Once, I went to the cellar and I was talking to the guy working at the cellar equipment and I asked him, "What are you doing?" and he said he was pressing the button. I asked, "Why do you press that button?" He didn't know – only that he needed to switch it on and off. He'd been doing

that for 20 years. I couldn't accept that people have to work for 20 years in the same environment not knowing how their job fits into the wider process at all.'

It's important to train cellar workers, Charl says, not only to give them pathways for personal growth, but also because they can often identify and prevent faults or spoilage in the winemaking process, resulting in cost savings.

GETTING INTO THE WINE BUSINESS

There are many career opportunities in the wine industry aside from winemaking: from research and academia to the export business, quality assurance, tasting and judging, sales, marketing, logistics, customer services, being a sommelier, tourism and finance. These are opportunities that more people need to know about. Regardless of one's background, there are many ways to make a career out of wine.

Winemaker Adi Badenhorst says the best way to get into the business is to dive in and get experience: 'Often people ask me where they can go and study to get into the wine business. I say the first thing that you must do is go and work on a farm. Work in a winery. Start, get a sense of the whole business. Get to know the people and the industry in that way.'

But Gillian Arendse says it's also important to celebrate and profile the stars who've made it in the industry. 'For me, it feels as if they're one in a billion. We need to find ways to position these people as individuals who've succeeded against the odds, and in doing so have been part of creating something bigger.'

NOTES
1   Booysen, J (21 June 2016): 'SA Wine Industry Could Add 100 000 Jobs by 2025', https://www. iol.co.za/business-report/economy/sa-wine-industry-could-add-100-000-jobs-by-2025-2036755 (accessed 4 June 2018).
2   Mama, M (3 January 2018): 'Black Youths Must be Made Aware of Agri Sector Careers', https:// www.farmersweekly.co.za/opinion/by-invitation/black-youths-must-made-aware-agri-sector-careers/(accessed 4 June 2018).
3   Swanepoel, E (1 August 2017): 'The Real Matric Marks', *City Press* https://www.news24.com/ SouthAfrica/News/the-real-matric-marks-20170107 (accessed 11 June 2018).
4   Ibid.
5   McCarthy, J and Oliphant, R (October 2013): 'Mathematics Outcomes in South African Schools: What Are the Facts? What Should be Done?', Centre for Development and Enterprise, https://www.cde.org.za/wp-content/uploads/2013/10/MATHEMATICS%20 OUTCOMES%20IN%20SOUTH%20AFRICAN%20SCHOOLS.pdf (accessed 4 June 2018).
6   South African Wine Industry Information and Systems (30 January 2015): 'Macro-economic Impact of the Wine Industry on the South African Economy', http://www.sawis.co.za/info/ download/Macro-economic_impact_study_-_Final_Report_Version_4_30Jan2015.pdf (accessed 4 June 2018).

Dumisani Mathonsi in the laboratory at Stellenbosch University.

TASTING WINE

'We need to break down the intimidation factor. I was tasting a wine and someone said it tasted like truffles. I thought they meant chocolate. So this chef took me into the kitchen and made me smell truffles and truffle oil, and as I smelled it I said, "This smells like the milk at the bottom of a calabash." You need to associate the smell and taste with things that are familiar.'
— *Ntsiki Biyela, winemaker*

'One barrier to the consumption of wine is the names of wines themselves. If you're unfamiliar with wine, how do you know whether a Cabernet Sauvignon is a type of wine or a type of grape, or whether it's sweet or dry? You can tell the colour and very little else from the label of a bottle of wine. It's a barrier to consumers trying to come into the market. On the other hand, it also contributes to the enhanced status of wine.'
— *Michael Fridjhon, wine writer*

'The tasting terms can be frightening. A guy noses a wine and says, "Ah, tastes like loganberries." What's a loganberry? People talk of minerality when they describe wine. What does that mean? These terms can be quite off-putting. Everyone needs to find their own point of reference and use terms that people can identify with.'
— *Adi Badenhorst, winemaker*

'I had never tasted wine before and then the company I worked for sent me on an introduction to wine course, where we learned to taste different wines. At first I wasn't used to the taste and found it very bitter: it kind of bit you in the mouth! But I developed my palate to really appreciate the complexity of what I was tasting in the bottle. We need to educate consumers so that they don't feel intimidated to try something different, instead of just taking the brands that they know.'
— *Vernon Henn, wine producer*

THE BUSINESS OF WINE

MNIKELO MANGCIPHU

A SOWETO WINE MERCHANT

I don't measure my achievement by how many bottles of wine I've sold, but by how many people understand wine better and come back for more.

Morara Wine, which opened in 2005, was Soweto's first boutique wine and spirits shop. We stock over a hundred wine labels, ranging from easy drinking to good value and expensive brands. The walls are stacked from floor to ceiling with an array of South African wines: John Carlou, Nederburg, Kanonkop and Fairview.

The shop is located in Mofolo, once the home of Soweto's more affluent population. When you told people you lived in Mofolo, they looked up to you. In 1978 we boasted Soweto's first proper cinema – Eyethu. I often walked there to watch a movie. I saw *The Good, The Bad and the Ugly*, *The Ten Commandments* and my favourite, *Jaws*.

Things changed in the mid-1980s when migrants moved into the hostels and shack dwellers took over parts of Mofolo. But it's still a vibrant suburb, boasting restaurants and pubs and Mofolo Park where regular jazz events take place. Across the street from my shop is a local car-tyre place, a carwash and a woman selling fruit and vegetables by the side of the road.

And there's something else, something unusual about my shop. There are no steel bars here. Most stores selling liquor in Soweto sell from behind metal bars. But I feel safe because this is my community. The shop is down the road from the house where I grew up. Everyone knows me.

Wine is something new and can be intimidating, but I'm introducing it around people I know. That makes a big difference. If you know a place it's easier to influence change.

My father died when I was four years old. My mother supported all of us – my three sisters and me – on her nurse's salary, and because she had to work night shifts we were sometimes sent to live with our grandmother in Emdeni.

At the age of 16, I got caught up in the June 1976 student uprising. On 15 June, we heard rumours that we were marching to Pretoria the next day to protest the

introduction of Afrikaans into schools. I arrived at school on 16 June and students were chanting 'Khulula uMandela' – release Mandela so he can come speak on our behalf. I joined in and then from nowhere three nyalas shot teargas at us. I was next to my friend Barry. Suddenly a stray bullet hit Barry behind the ear and I watched my friend die in front of me.

My friends and I had to walk 20 kilometres home because there was no transport. Burned cars and trucks littered the streets. Just before we reached Mofolo, one of the guys suggested that we go loot the local bottle store, which was associated with the hated West Rand Administration Board – a symbol of apartheid repression. So we ran to the Dube bottle store and took two cases of Viceroy brandy, which we buried under a tree in our yard. Then we returned to the street to drink some of our spoils. That day was the first time I had alcohol. I got completely drunk and when darkness fell, I was trapped. Was it worse to stay on the street and risk being picked up by the security police, or to go home and face my mother?

My mother found me and dragged me home, and my sister told her about the hidden alcohol in the yard. She forced me to dig up every bottle and then poured it all down the drain. Like many young township boys, I didn't go back to school. I loitered for four years. I wanted to join my friends and neighbours who were going into exile but I didn't want to leave my mother alone. I was the man of the house.

I couldn't find work and it was the days of boycotts. We would wait at the entrance to the township and stop people going to work or buying goods in the city.

My mother was scared for me and sent me away to relatives in Nelspruit. There, I bunked school for a year. I never liked school and just went to please my mom. And I missed the township. My friends were fighting the regime and I was stuck in Nelspruit!

'There's something else, something unusual about my shop. There are no steel bars here. Most stores selling liquor in Soweto sell from behind metal bars. But I feel safe because this is my community.'

Finally, at 22, I came back to Soweto to finish matric. After that a friend who'd left the country helped me get a United Nations scholarship to study in Lesotho, where I did a four-year diploma in accounting. I returned home and spent the next eight years working in the meat business. I got married and moved to Pretoria.

It was during this time that I first became acquainted with wine. More than the taste, I fell in love with the people who were drinking it. They were chilled and calm. I wanted to be like them. I registered for a one-year part-time course on South African wines with the Cape Wine Academy.

One day I was having a drink with a friend who had a mug that said 'Soweto Beer Festival' and it came to me – we should have a Soweto Wine Festival. So, through a friend, I approached Marilyn Cooper, then the CEO of the Cape Wine Academy. I knew I needed support because if I tried to start a project like this, no wine farm would buy my story. They had this perception that wine isn't for black people. But she loved the idea.

So the Soweto Wine Festival was born, a partnership between Marilyn Cooper and myself. It's a platform for people from Soweto to come and experience wines, to grow black consumers. But the first festival, in 2004 at the Ubuntu Kraal in Orlando West, wasn't a success. We had about 1 500 visitors over three days. We hadn't really explained what the event was about and people came because it was a cheap way to get drunk. They didn't see it as an opportunity to learn about wine and interact with winemakers from different wineries. This upset many exhibitors who weren't keen to return, but I wasn't giving up.

I persuaded wine farms and owners that we had to support each other. Changing mindsets takes time. If we made it work, it would address all our bottom lines. We wanted to get it right, to promote wine and responsible drinking too. And we did get it right – 12 years later the Soweto Wine Festival is now an annual event.

Morara Wine, which was inspired by the Soweto Wine Festival, gives people a space to come and ask questions about wine and learn to enjoy it. I knew when I started out that there wasn't a ready-made market for my new business. Wine isn't a drink of choice for black people. I knew when I ventured into this that there was a whole lot of work to be done to cultivate the market. Traditionally we're spirits, cider and beer drinkers. Many people have negative perceptions about wine – that it's for whites, it's elitist.

About four years ago some guy came to the shop and he wanted some advice on what kind of wine to buy. I asked him what he enjoyed – do you have a sweet palate? Do you want something more dry? He said he was buying it for his girlfriend, so to just give him something sweet. Later I discovered that he was buying it for himself. He was embarrassed to tell me that, because in our community if you're a black man seen to be drinking wine, you're labelled a sissy.

Customers who used to say, 'Give me red wine,' now come into Morara Wine and Spirits Emporium and ask for a Pinotage or a Shiraz. For me, this represents progress. I feel great pride when people who came through the door five years ago asking for a box of sweet wine now say, 'Mnikelo, I think I want to try a new blend. What do you recommend?' This is what changing the mindset of a community is all about.

'Traditionally we're spirits, cider and beer drinkers. Many people have negative perceptions about wine – that it's for whites, it's elitist.'

NKULULEKO MKHWANAZI

AN UNEXPECTED CAREER

I love the complexity of wine. I love that in each glass there's a story and sense of a place.

I grew up in Umlazi, in KwaZulu-Natal. I first got interested in wine when I was 16 or 17 years old. When my father drank wine with his friends, they were always animated. They'd hold the glass up and talk about how special this vintage was compared to that one; it made me curious.

After school I went to the University of Cape Town (UCT) to do Philosophy, Politics and Economics (PPE), and during orientation week I joined the UCT wine club. We met every Friday night and tasted wines. On weekends we went to wine farms. That's where my interest really started. I went and did an introductory wine course through the Cape Wine Academy.

When I left university I wasn't really sure what to do. I wanted to do something different. It never occurred to me that wine could be a career option. I got a job working in restaurants and really enjoyed selling wine. So I decided to try to stay in the industry and make it my career.

People are always more open to buying wine if they can taste it first, so I host different wine events. I tell them the story of the wine. That is very important. You aren't just selling a bottle of wine, you're selling a story about a winemaker and the place it comes from.

I'm currently working as a wine ambassador for Creation Wines and other brands. I do their marketing and sales. I run a wine company called Shamase and we're in the process of developing a wine brand in partnership with a Cape wine estate. I hope my wine will be ready in 2019.

Another leg of the company is the Shamase Wine Club, which creates a relaxed environment, mainly for young black professionals who want to understand more about wine. The Club offers monthly tastings in Durban and Johannesburg. The idea is to get people out of their comfort zones and excited to be adventurous and try new wines. There are so many wines to choose from and it's sometimes difficult to know where to begin. It's not like beer or gin, where you have your brand and you stick to it.

In 2011, I was accepted to the Michael Fridjhon Wine Judging Academy, a really exciting turning point in my career. The Academy's role is to introduce new young judges to the industry. It was extremely intense and pretty intimidating. We had different presenters, like Gary Jordan from Jordan Wines. We had to identify wines from France, New Zealand, Spain and South Africa. It took place over three days and in that time we tasted about 350 wines. We would taste 10 or 20 wines at a time. We obviously had to spit afterwards otherwise we wouldn't still be standing by the end of the day!

It was structured like a wine competition. There was continuous time pressure and we had to taste very quickly, make notes, give the wine a score and then move on to the next one. There were also sessions on older wines and we tasted about 30 Bordeaux blends. There you had to identify not only the wine but the year as well, and pick up the nuances of the different wines and then judge them. I was one of four students who achieved a distinction.

I was thrilled when I got invited to the 2011 Old Mutual Trophy Wine Show as an associate judge. It was such an honour to be a judge in the same room as people like Hong Kong-based Master of Wine Debra Meiburg, Christian Eedes, editor of *WineMag*, and industry veteran Michael Fridjhon.

The competition had its lighter moments. A 'no-name' brand from a local retailer, which sold for R35, ended up winning a trophy. It was really controversial but it shows that it's a pretty fair process – all wines are given a fair chance. I went back and tasted that R35 bottle and it was a well-made wine and a well-deserved winner.

I was a judge at the Old Mutual Trophy Wine Show for four years running. I learned a lot and became more confident as a senior judge. I hope to judge internationally in the future.

Some of my friends think I'm crazy. They tell me I like to drink, so why do I call it work? They still drink mainly beer but I've managed to convert them and now they appreciate a glass or two of good wine too.

'You aren't just selling a bottle of wine, you're selling a story about a winemaker and the place it comes from.'

MICHAEL FRIDJHON

JUDGING WINE

The business of wine assessment isn't uncontroversial, and whether the judgement is made to produce ratings, award medals or simply describe a wine's qualities, the exercise is fraught with difficulties.

A problem common to any attempt at aesthetic appreciation is objectivity. Value-free opinions are rare outside the world of abstract mathematics. And objectivity is pretty much impossible when the subject matter relates solely to the response of the five senses to sensory input.

Smell and taste are inherently subjective. My idea of spicy may taste bland to you. Likewise, what I think is medium-sweet could be almost too dry for another palate. The same difficulties afflict other sensory elements too: how red is the red wine, how pale is the white? Is the yellow colour of an oak-aged Chardonnay still fresh or showing signs of oxidation? One man's 'plush and rich' may well be another's 'harsh and austere'.

This minefield of qualitative judgement isn't limited to wine. It's to be found through-out the world of the arts and in some respects it's present wherever judgement – rather than simply factual verification – is involved.

During the three days of the wine-judging course at the Michael Fridjhon Wine Judging Academy, we expose people to a range of wines, local and international, that we hope will help them to refine their ideas about wine quality. Sometimes the same – or very similar – wines are presented in two different contexts, which helps to illustrate the relative nature of appreciation (although hopefully not of judgement). Illustration and example, rather than commentary, are pretty much the way the course works, so that almost all the sessions are conducted around tastings.

The course also deals with wine faults, the one area of aesthetic judgement where an element of objectivity is possible. Knowing, identifying and understanding what causes certain defects, and how they're likely to evolve, is crucial to a full assessment of the product.

Some winemaking faults utterly ruin all the work of the grape grower. Cellar taints – which present as mouldy notes and corky whiffs – are the least controversial. Volatile acidity can add an extra dimension but usually indicates premature deterioration. Some faults, like the discernible presence of brettanomyces, a spoilage yeast that gives a wine an elastoplast aroma, are tolerated by some judges and rejected by others. However, until you're able to identify it for what it is, you can't make a complete assessment.

Most importantly, however, the course tries to teach an aesthetic based on drink-ability, refinement, complexity, integrity and persistence. This may seem a self-evident selection of taste criteria but it's by no means one that's universally embraced.

Wines, like all other 'created' works of art, are the artefacts of intention. Winemakers talk of how they're merely the midwives of the terroir, of the place where the grapes have grown, but every decision they take moves inexorably towards the end result.

In the end, judging wine isn't about a fixed or magical number; the score, whether in points or stars, is merely an approval rating. It's about recognising what the winemaker intended to achieve, assessing the wisdom of that decision, and quantifying how successfully the end result reflects what he or she set out to do.

'Smell and taste are inherently subjective. My idea of spicy may taste bland to you. Likewise, what I think is medium-sweet could be almost too dry for another palate.'

RAYMOND NDLOVU

FROM STOCKBROKER TO WINE PRODUCER

The wine business is fascinating. You meet a diverse range of people from all walks of life. It's an incredibly vibrant and colourful world.

I was a stockbroker for nearly three decades and got into the wine business through a fortunate coincidence.

At the end of 2011, my partner Kevin Swart and I sold our joint stockbroking business. He moved from Johannesburg down to Franschhoek and bought a smallholding property with a vineyard. He invited me to join him and it wasn't long before I decided to also leave Johannesburg and move here with my family. I was tired of the finance world and ready for something new.

We made the decision to move to Franschhoek on a whim, with no real clue as to what was to follow. We went into partnership with winemaker Jacques Wentzel, and Black Elephant Vintners was born.

What we weren't prepared for were the reactions to our decision to move to this quaint village. Regardless of people's backgrounds, our decision to make Franschhoek our home, let alone invest in the wine industry, still draws sighs of bemused disbelief and curiosity.

So much of the wine business is about process, which you never appreciate in the fast-paced and unrelenting world of finance. You learn to work with Mother Nature and submit to her timeless process.

You never know what to expect from any vintage. When the grapes are ready to harvest, you have one opportunity, and that's part of the intrigue and allure of being in this business. However, it's also a complicated industry and I'm constantly learning. Winemaking isn't a singular thing. You work with multiple suppliers, including the different vineyards from which we source our grapes. It's about building lasting and fruitful partnerships with people. And, of course, aiming always to create the best possible product.

The challenges are not insignificant. The nature of the industry is that you're always fighting a working capital cycle. Your cash is tied into what you see in the barrels and the

tanks, and it takes a long time (two to three years) before you can turn that cash into income and, eventually, sustained profits.

As new entrants to the industry, we found it easy to approach it like any other business. Our business experience informed the capital-light initial investment and streamlined business model, with limited overheads. We combined basic business principles with the science of making wine and the art of experiencing the brand and consuming the wine.

Our model is to outsource non-core processes and business activities, for example, on the production side in terms of sourcing grapes from different producers on contract. We rent a large cellar in the vicinity, which enables us to scale our production volumes as and when we choose. We have established partnerships with a number of marketing and distribution agents, both in South Africa and internationally.

Both Kevin and I have a natural flair for marketing, branding and storytelling, which has stood us in good stead in positioning Black Elephant Vintners as a fun, unconventional and bold experiential brand, a kind of 'rebels of the vine'.

We took the approach to grow slowly from home first. We wanted to be well known in our local market, starting here in Franschhoek, which is known as a food and wine capital of the country. We started by marketing our wines to local restaurants and guesthouses where there's a constant flow of local and international tourists. From there, we extended our market to Cape Town and to the rest of the country, including Gauteng, KwaZulu-Natal and the Eastern Cape. We've also established sales channels in Namibia, Zimbabwe, Zambia and Ghana. Our steady expansion into overseas markets encompasses the USA, the UK, the Netherlands, Germany, Denmark and Austria.

We're optimistic about the future of the South African wine industry in general and Black Elephant Vintners in particular. I never set out to be in the wine industry – but here I am. I'm happy to be a trailblazer. And, so far, we're grateful for the road less travelled.

TEBELLO MOTSOANE

THE WORLD OF PARTIES AND ENTERTAINMENT

There are lots of stereotypes about wine and black people. We don't understand wine. We drink cheap wine. We drink wine when we're broke. These are all misconceptions.

I'm from Katlehong, a township 35km east of Johannesburg, but I've always been a Joburg guy. After school I went to Wits university to do media studies and international relations. I started to throw parties to earn some money and that's where it all began.

From the parties I started managing DJs and developing artists. Then I learned about brands and sponsorships, and today I run a company called ShowLove, with clients that include Macallan Whisky and Capitec Bank. I love the world of entertainment and parties.

My interest in wine started through food. I've always enjoyed cooking shows. Those guys on the TV always had a glass of wine in the kitchen and always looked so cool.

I also enjoy cooking at home – I love meat and, in my opinion, a medium-rare ostrich steak with a glass of Shiraz is simply perfect. I don't think there are rules for pairing food and wine. You like what you like. You don't have to be scientific about it.

I didn't grow up drinking wine. I figured out what I like just by drinking and trying new brands. I read up on wine and visited places like Paarl and Franschhoek. I listened, learned and noticed how people consumed it.

I always wanted to go deeper into the wine business and in 2017 an opportunity came my way. I was approached by Kamogelo Kgadima, who worked as procurement and stock controller at Wildekrans Wine Estate in the Botrivier Valley. Braam Gericke, the winemaker, and Kamogelo initially wanted me to be an ambassador for their wine brands and run influencer campaigns on social media – they wanted to explore putting a face to the Wildekrans brand.

I went down to the farm and spent time with them and we got to know each other. We just clicked. I was interested in having my own wine brand and we started to discuss a different kind of partnership. I didn't want to own a wine farm – I wanted to work this end of the supply chain to market a product I'd helped develop and believe in.

We explored the idea of creating a unique South African sparkling wine, a Méthode Cap Classique (MCC). Over the next months, we tasted, talked and shared ideas. I learned so much. Usually MCC is made with Chardonnay but we decided to make ours with Chenin. So Atelier sparkling wine was born – a partnership between Wildekrans Wine Estate and myself. I created the label, the story, the look and feel, and developed a marketing strategy using the website, social media and different kinds of events.

Spending time with Braam in the beautiful Botrivier Valley was hugely rewarding too. As I kid I'd never been to the Western Cape – I grew up in Katlehong and never noticed or cared about nature. I'm a concrete guy! But from visiting Wildekrans I got to learn about nature: rainfall patterns, harvests, and how nature affects the growing grapes.

I got to love the sense of craft and process about wine. You can have the same grape and the same barrels, but you can have different wines because two winemakers added something different.

The wine business reminds me of the music industry. You can't create a great song and then sit and wait for a record label to approach you, a producer to find you or a radio station to play your song. You have to create your own platforms to push your products.

I love the names of wine brands. They add to the mystique. I don't think we should popularise it and make it less intimidating. Wine is like the mountain: if you want to climb it, you must go to it.

In terms of advertising, you see more for beer brands and spirits. There's a culture to wine that isn't mass media. Drinking wine is different to having a shot at the bar. If you order wine, you have to talk too. Wine and conversation always go hand in hand.

But wine is definitely becoming a popular leisure drink among the emerging black middle class. If I have an important meeting I'll always drink wine, not beer. It's an age thing, too – when I was 19, I used to drink whisky with Coke. Not any more!

In terms of black consumers, we're first-generation wealth right now and we're trying to figure out what we like and what we can afford. But you can't attach a price to quality, either. There are some great cheap wines and there are wines that are really expensive that I don't enjoy at all.

In terms of tasting wines, there's the suggested way: the nose, the swirl, the colour, whether you decant or not. I do all of that when I'm on a date and I'm trying to be fancy. When your date asks you why you're doing that and you break it down, she's always impressed. I wouldn't do it at home by myself. Short of drinking it straight out the bottle – I just pour.

With wine, the main thing is if you enjoy it. If you do – that's the one. If it tastes good, then great. If not, just try a different one.

WINE AND WORK

'Wine is a great social lubricant. In Bulgaria they say there isn't a problem that can't be solved over a glass of wine. I enjoy wine for its taste but also for the enjoyment of drinking wine with people.'
— *Bongiwe Njobe, former director-general, Department of Agriculture*

'Coming from a family of teetotallers, I never drank alcohol. Even when I was a student at university, I used to be the designated driver. After graduating I worked at the Durban Port in economic research and marketing. It was the early 1990s, a time when South Africa was coming of age. Sanctions had been dropped and trade was picking up. A guy I was working with said to me, "Sithembiso, if you want to get ahead in this space, you've got to be prepared to go out to eat and enjoy wine with clients." That's when I realised I needed to learn about wine. It's a taste I acquired over time and learned to love.'
— *Sithembiso Mthethwa, director, Kalipha Foundation*

THE FUTURE OF WINE

THE
NEXT GLASS

LOOKING BACK, AND FORWARDS

JOHN PLATTER

Why has South Africa, a significant wine producer for centuries with, lately, beautiful wines enjoying unprecedented international acclaim, never developed a wine culture much beyond the confines of the Cape Winelands and certainly not among 80% of the population, the black community?

'As everyone in wine knows, to make a fortune you need to start with a bigger one. '

People everywhere were smiling. Some in the queue looked a bit unsure: how would things change? But every eye contact drew a smile. The sky was clearing. Could it clear away 342 years of the stormiest of histories?

There we all were, in a long line snaking through a Stellenbosch vineyard on the morning of 27 April 1994. Some in their Sunday best, others in overalls. Equal votes. The first free election.

My wife Erica and I had come down from our patch of vines on the Helderberg. The sun shone brightly and we needed our wide hats. Four hours went by until we reached the booth.

Nelson Mandela's Long Road to here was incomplete, we knew, but where was it leading to? What now? Could it be a place where, one day, if we and others tried our best, we could dream of the privilege of not always thinking about race?

Cape wine was white-owned and had been, always. And after a quarter of a century we still ask, what now? What explains this and the many other problems now besetting the struggling Cape wine industry?

More than half of its 3 200 grape growers are either already under water financially or on the knife edge of derisory 1% returns on investment – mirroring, roughly, the national economic growth rate. For the past decade, a hundred farmers a year have been leaving or diversifying out of the wine business. The Cape exports nearly half of its annual wine production and 60% of that is shipped in bulk, fetching the lowest commodity prices of any wine-producing country in the world.

A century ago, in January 1918, the KWV acquired government statutory powers to regulate production with strictly-enforced quotas and pricing – a classic, mainly ethnic (white, Afrikaner) cartel that lasted for the best part of the twentieth century. It provided a privileged but also distorted 'stability' – emasculated, eventually, by international anti-apartheid boycotts that excluded Cape wine from one of the most exciting, expansive periods in wine's long history.

From the 1970s, 'New World' wine producers – Australia, New Zealand, California, Chile, Argentina and others; our competitors – rose to challenge the long, staid hegemony of the 'Old World' pretentiousness of France, Italy, Germany and Spain, with sheer quality, fresher and cleaner wines, uninhibited marketing and labelling exuberance. The surge in wine quality everywhere left South Africa scrambling to catch up. Trade boycotts in the 1980s becalmed the industry, reducing it to shipping quality wine in bulk.

Eventually, the Mandela transition to democracy in 1994 ended the boycotts. Exports soared exponentially, initially mainly to the UK and Europe, but finally to 110 countries.

Today, premium-quality Cape wines hold their own with confidence internationally. From 850 wineries – 7 500 labels each vintage – there's enough excitement to attract sustained tributes from international authorities like Jancis Robinson, Robert Parker and Tim Atkin; Atkin says South Africa is 'among the world's most dynamic and exciting wine producers'. Acclaim such as 'best fine wines for your money' from *The Wall Street Journal* are now gratifyingly monotonous in their frequency. We take a *Decanter* cover announcing Upper Hemel-en-Aarde Valley Newton Johnson Pinot Noir as the 'Pinot of the Year' in our stride.

The trouble is, as in all wine countries, top quality – real money-making quality – constitutes a small percentage of the total production, in South Africa's case probably less than about 5% commanding R500 or more per bottle. Labels in this exalted category probably number fewer than a hundred, among them those from family-owned estates, lightly-geared and tightly-run but also including artisanal garagistes making a few barrels in a year for fun or artistic kudos, requiring some skill but little capital.

As everyone in wine knows, to make a fortune you need to start with a bigger one. Serious new investors – chiefly from Germany, France and the USA – include the ego-driven seeking smart addresses and showcase restaurants. In the past 20 years they've become key contributors, like wildlife lodges and game reserves, to South Africa's tourist attractions.

CONSUME, CONSUME, CONSUME

Unfortunately for the wine industry, beer remains the national drink of South Africa. Its brands attract the kind of loyal following unknown to wine and put the country among the world's top 20 alcohol consumers.

There are signs that a few categories of wine – sparkling, semi-sweet and even Cabernet and Chardonnay – are winning favour. But to make a real difference would mean appreciably lifting the low overall domestic wine consumption from about ten litres per capita a year. In France and Spain it's 43 litres.

There are new initiatives to change these consumption statistics, however. If the mood takes him after a glass of wine or two, Aubrey Ngcungama can entertain a party with a window-rattling tenor's piece from the opera of your choice. We're having morning coffee with some leading lights of BLACC, the Black Cellar Club, in Cape Town's The Stack restaurant. The members are a recently-formed brother- and sisterhood in the hospitality business. They taste together once a week, exchanging ideas on everything from humouring guests to venting about employers, and how to fend off eager wine producers keen to get wines listed.

BLACC members collectively are now powerful arbiters of ever-changing wine lists at Cape Town's restaurants. Their tastes matter.

Membership has taken off – countrywide nearly 1 300. BLACC aims to spread Africa-wide. Wine estates charter buses to fetch members for wineland trips and special tastings. Plans to stage wine festivals in townships like Langa are in advanced stages.

The big question: why are so many black people still wine resistant – price, taste, mystery? They're unanimous: it's changing.

How so?

'Well,' says Aubrey, 'perhaps because they're hearing the message from those of us with the same funny skin colour.'

Is membership confined to black people?

'Definitely not,' he says. 'We're done with segregation.'

Trevor Gower of Meander Fine Wines in the KwaZulu-Natal Midlands is picking up similar signals. 'Our black clients used to buy expensive labels,' he says. 'They've begun to experiment: they're more confident in their own tastes, and buying not on label or reputation but what they like, even if it's quite cheap.'

Michael Fridjhon stages wine events not only in the major cities, but also in East London and Mpumalanga. They're attended now by many more black patrons and he reports that delighted exclamations praising 'iChardonnay' and 'iCabernet' ring around the halls. Pleasure and knowledge are spreading. Black people are drinking more wine, and while wine-estate ownership remains virtually white, many of wine's ancillary businesses are transforming, and a crop of new farm-partnership models are providing a more vested black interest in wine production.

That said, after 24 years of democracy, of a total of 95 000 hectares of vineyards, only an estimated 2 500 hectares (2,6%) are black-owned; the African Farmers' Association says, overall, less than 1% of Cape farms are owned by black people. These are perfect stats for the raised voices clamouring for land expropriation without compensation.

Not least among the multiple challenges to Cape wine are the inexorable forces of nature – droughts, water restrictions and climate warming. They're beginning to nudge vineyard re-plantings farther up mountainsides and towards the cooler maritime rim.

Diversification (tomatoes, blueberries, nuts, citrus) and industry consolidations will reconfigure Cape agriculture and wine in the next decade, sometimes brutally. Some 50 farms in Stellenbosch are said to be for sale. On the line will be some of the 290 000 jobs in wine and the annual R36-billion contribution to the GDP (1,2% of total).

Diversifying out of vineyards may improve the province's agricultural profitability but the fiscus will miss wine's 'sin tax' contribution. In 2017, the state earned R5,78 billion in excise duty and VAT; primary producers grossed R4,79 billion.

The Cape wine scene is on the threshold of immense change – and that's without the rising political heat around land reform and expropriation.

Smaller wine crops (20–30% down in 2018) and shortages may provide pricing upticks, producer respites and periods of relative stability, but a long-term movement to fewer vineyards, less wine and finer quality at higher prices seems likely. It's a healthier business

27 April 1994, all South Africans queue together to vote for the first time.

model, perhaps – and reverses centuries of a brandy and wine industry concerned more with grapes in quantity than quality – but with important social consequences.

Are there the shafts of optimism, of hopeful sunshine breaking through these emotionally-charged scenarios?

PIONEERS

Unathi Mantshongo seems to glide over her achievements and the significance of her key role in the Cape wine scene. She wasn't parachuted into the white and male-dominated preserve; she worked her way up.

Oenology and viticulture were unknowns to Mthatha-born Unathi when she found herself at Stellenbosch University, then, and still, predominantly an Afrikaans-speaking institution. The town is the spiritual heart of the historic Cape Winelands, shadowed by soaring mountains; vines creep into the oak-lined streets with their whitewashed Cape-Dutch gables and sprawling university buildings. The country's second-oldest settlement, it occupies a rarefied, privileged world apart.

The all-pervading wine milieu didn't weaken Unathi's initial no-alcohol resolve. After three years, when she needed to start tasting wine for work, she found it so 'terrible I couldn't believe people were drinking it'.

What captivated Unathi about viticulture, she says, was how 'for all the science in the world, Mother Nature decides'. How the vines behave and how the wine turns out each year depends on variables beyond the winemaker's skills to control. That tickled her. And her mood and expression soften as she speaks of sitting on hillside vineyards among the mountains, enjoying the fresh air. So the girl from Mthatha, with good maths and science grades, was drawn into the strange worldwide fellowship of wine.

'Actually,' says the once-teetotalling Unathi with a giggle, now ten years after completing her honours, 'I'm probably drinking a bit too much wine these days.' It might be entirely uncoincidental that her Italian partner hails from Veneto in northern Italy, a region steeped in vino-centric cuisine.

Her story, and those of her colleagues Dumisani Mathonsi, Ntsiki Biyela and Carmen Stevens, is about breaking into the world of Cape wine, another culture. They're pioneers moving into the exclusive preserves of South African wine, claiming some of the glamour and the money as cellarmasters, viticulturists and wine merchants.

The Colour of Wine documentary film chronicles, frankly and in their own words, how some of these hesitant, sometimes bewildered but smart newcomers struggled and eventually succeeded. Others didn't: they changed courses or dropped out; and others still, including some of the brightest and most promising, qualified but then left wine.

'It's not possible to see this film and not feel ashamed,' wrote Michael Fridjhon, South Africa's most incisive wine writer, in *Wine* magazine. He'd worked hard with Jabulani Ntshangase to find openings and bursaries and provide support for the SAA Wine Education Bursary set up in 1994. 'One glimpse at who is in charge of the country's production facilities – now in 2017 – tells a story of a lack of transformation that is not a matter of coincidence but a monument to a concerted effort which starts at the top and permeates down – from the generally white male heads of quasi-statutory institutions all the way to the employers who appoint cellarmasters and viticulturists. The wall of white faces that greeted the heroes of *The Colour of Wine* when they set out in the 1990s is largely unchanged.'

SKILL – THE MOST POTENT GAME-CHANGER

From the outset, everyone understood that racial transformation through real estate or land ownership, its running costs, the long financial horizons and low profit margins, were beyond easy reach. High-level skills were the most potent and accessible game-changers – but the slowest to acquire.

The former vice chancellor of the University of Cape Town, Dr Mamphela Ramphele, said, 20 years into democracy, that though it was a 'gutter education' under apartheid, it's even worse now: '80% of schools are failing'. Universities, she says, are reduced to an 'ambulance service', rescuing survivors of South African schools.

Ask hard-nosed Burgundy-raised and -trained international wine-trade veteran Alex Dale, of Radford Dale in Stellenbosch, what the hold-up is and why transformation is taking so long, and he'll give you a one-word answer: education. It's been a singular failure. 'Simply distributing land isn't going to work. If you gave me farms free tomorrow to start off previously disadvantaged people, it would be suicide. This business is tough enough if you know what you're doing; the market is incredibly brutal.'

The Radford Dale Land of Hope Trust wine range, managed by the Land of Hope trustees, is an investment in the education of their children. Using the winery's facilities to make their own brand wines, they export to the UK, Netherlands, Canada and Poland.

Black economic empowerment black-white partnership deals – some mere window-dressing stitch-ups – might have offered elaborate deal-making and quick-fix equity opportunities. But they began floundering early and didn't include skills along with equity transfers. Continuous project evaluation, with expert advisory services on tap, should have been – but, incredibly, still is not – a mandatory, integral part of all transformation projects in South African agriculture.

It's ironic that despite the prospect of more droughts, which in 2018 have reduced harvests by 20–30%, South Africa is producing some of the finest wines, and in the richest diversity of styles, in its 366-year-long history. The beauty, elegance, clarity and purity of fruit, and the delicate balance and range of styles of these wines, from so many different regions and so many new names, is simply enchanting.

The past decade has seen an explosion of daring departures and innovation with new (to South Africa) varieties or old, revived vineyards in previously unfashionable regions. These include 'legacy' wines from Old Vines fruit, a project spearheaded by viticulturist Rosa Kruger. Rosa has compiled a national treasury of more than 3 000 hectares of ancient, low-production vines, whose continued existence relies on high boutique prices from artisanal producers.

Many of these 'New Frontier' wines are made by young, landless, highly qualified, well-travelled, internationally attuned entrepreneurs, without significant capital,

'It's ironic that despite the prospect of more droughts, which in 2018 have reduced harvests by 20-30%, South Africa is producing some of the finest wines.'

benchmarking themselves against the big names of the wine world. They're eager, locally, to outshine the landed estate gentry and established brands.

After the decades of pre-1994 international trade boycotts and ostracism, there are now reasons for national pride. The awkward news is that the adventurous new quality flagbearers of today – some produce no more than a few barrels a vintage – probably don't constitute even 1% of South Africa's annual production of 1,2 million tons. However, such 'statement' wines, priced at above R400 and even up to R1 000 a bottle, lift the country's wine image. The most ambitious now breach the R4 000 mark, and are obviously not made for the domestic consumer. At those prices, they're competing with the prestigious names of Europe.

So they're a prized counterpoint to South Africa's image-lowering overall export prices. Our slack domestic consumption forces South Africa to export 50% of its approximate annual 1 000-million-litre production, 60% of which goes cheaply in bulk to be bottled abroad. It's not a good business model, and for the commercial, commodity producers, increasingly a hazardous one. The nature of the wine business provides space, alongside the commercial, for crafted, brilliant talking-point, optimistic exceptions to keep the South African wine flag fluttering.

THE AU PAIR WHO LOST HER WAY – A REMARKABLE MENTORSHIP

Mentorship, once but no longer a dirty word implying paternalism, is now widely accepted as indispensable in what is a modern, intricate, scientific business.

Meet Berene Sauls, the au pair who lost her way. 'I think I was too militaristic with their daughters and I was sacked after a month,' she says. 'I actually wanted to join the army; I come from a strict family.' She's from an obscure village in the hills behind Hermanus, Tesselaarsdal, where in 1810 a white settler left his property to freed slaves – Berene's forebears.

The daughters Berene had to care for were the Hamilton Russell children at Anthony Hamilton Russell's vineyards in the Hemel-en-Aarde, long respected throughout the world of wine for their fine Pinot Noirs and Chardonnays. 'Berene was just too bright, so we offered her a job in the winery,' Anthony clarifies.

Berene eventually took charge of the exports, managing the tediously legal hoops of excise and VAT, wine certifications, separate labelling requirements for different export regions, and marshalling shipping agents. But she's an irrepressible, laughing, inquisitive woman, all hustle and bustle – and she wouldn't keep her nose out of the winery.

Berene couldn't use grapes for her own wine from the Hamilton Russell vineyards – they scarcely produced enough to meet their own demand – but Anthony accompanied her during her initial negotiations to buy in grapes from the Hemel-en-Aarde growers, and provided startup finance. A young coloured woman with no formal winemaking training and not much of a bank account would have been at a disadvantage. 'With Anthony at the table, they listened,' says Berene.

Winemaker Berene Sauls with her 2018 vintage.

She rented space in the Hamilton Russell Vineyards cellar and Emul Ross, among South Africa's most respected young winemakers, was as keen to share his skills as Berene was to learn them.

The Pinot Noir block of La Vierge Babylon vineyards on the Hemel-en-Aarde ridge, where Berene buys her grapes to produce Tesselaarsdal Pinot Noir.

Now the failed au pair has her own Tesselaarsdal Pinot Noir, which sells for R400–R500 a bottle, with a useful quantity going to the US. Growing and making Pinot Noir is a particularly intricate, painstaking challenge in wine.

'My wine,' says Berene with pride, 'is a bit fruitier than Anthony's; the grapes come from farther up the valley, from La Vierge, so it's good to have the distinction.' But in so many other respects, from the classic feel of the label and the premium choice of bottle, to the careful wording of the marketing information and website, the Hamilton Russell Vineyards mentorship leaves its unmistakable mark.

'On big occasions, when Anthony has important buyers and Masters of Wine here, he'll interrupt his own presentation to introduce me. I can explain my Tesselaarsdal and taste it with them but he's already pointed out the key people in the room whose names I must remember and who I need to make eye contact with,' says Berene. 'I've learned so much.'

She still handles the Hamilton Russell Vineyards exports but her own modest operation in three vintages has sailed past R1,4-million-a-year turnover.

'I do believe private enterprise can't sit back. It needs to be an active force, and work with government,' Anthony says. Education is key to transformation, he believes, which is why, in 1996, he founded a preschool on the farm, open to kids from neighbouring farms too.

The Tesselaarsdal 'model' of wine operation ticks six boxes: low setup costs, small exclusive quantities, brilliant wines, high prices, classy marketing, enthusiastic mentoring. Those who still wonder if this is a self-serving, paternalistic arrangement wouldn't want to hear Berene's colourful ripostes explaining *she's* the net winner.

Berene is now headed for an Elsenburg college wine and viticulture course, paid for by government. She's looking to buy a piece of land eventually, and perhaps plant her own vineyard at Tesselaarsdal.

FAIRVIEW: A HOUSE TO CALL YOUR OWN

In recent times, there hasn't been a more adventurous, out-of-the-box thinker and doer in the Cape Winelands than Charles Back of Fairview Wines at Paarl. His grandfather was a Lithuanian immigrant who landed, penniless, in the Cape in 1902.

Fairview is many things: a goat farm (of several breeds) and a producer of cheeses, while Angus beef cattle, pigs, fowl, trees and crops form a mostly self-sustaining food chain.

Twenty years ago, Back commissioned Stellenbosch sociologists, headed by Professor Joachim Ewert, to conduct a study of 48 employees. In the survey, the five most desirable life improvements they listed were a house to call their own (from which they couldn't be evicted), higher pay, a medical scheme, secure schooling nearby and a pension. Only one of them wanted land.

Mandela's first Minister of Agriculture and Land Affairs, Derek Hanekom, initiated a scheme in the late 1990s to settle labourers in their own homes, with government grants to buy homes on subdivided sections of farmland, on or off farms. It sounded like a win-win idea, and was certainly beneficial to labourers who lost their jobs and would otherwise suddenly find themselves homeless. So Back bought an adjoining piece of land to offer subdivisions and title deeds to his workers to purchase with the state grants they would receive. He also launched a gain-sharing scheme, a 'Fair Valley' range of wines,

TOP: *Berene in the vineyard.*
BOTTOM: *The village of Tesselaarsdal.*

utilising Fairview winery space and infrastructure.

The subdivision applications are still gathering dust in government pending trays 20 years later. Why? Because regional government wouldn't process the subdivisions of national-government schemes. The delay may also reflect the sharp turn under the Thabo Mbeki administration in favour of larger-scale and flashier restructuring of black economic empowerment deals. It seemed to regard smallholding ideas as 'soup-kitchen' palliatives that would entrench peasant poverty.

In early 2018, Hanekom heard of the holdup at Fairview. He'd been out of favour during Mbeki's presidency, later returning to serve in Jacob Zuma's revolving cabinets, to be sacked once again for daring to propose his president be fired. Now he was back at the Tourism ministry for President Cyril Ramaphosa (a position he had previously held), and he visited Fairview. Back was impressed that Hanekom owned up to the problem, and hoped that something would happen now.

Back's plan is to develop the Fair Valley project into a diverse, multi-purpose, residential, small-enterprise hub. His cousin Michael Back at the progressive nearby Backsberg Estate has also bought land nearby to establish a village where workers own their own homes.

PARTNERSHIPS WITH FARM WORKERS

Some farm workers have feelings of negativity about partnership arrangements with landowners, and it 'really comes down to a question of trust', says Ilse Ruthford, MD of Compagniesdrift, among the most promising and businesslike new 'transformation' models. Compagniesdrift is a bottling, packaging and storage business developed in 2015 by Meerlust Estate's Hannes Myburgh in partnership with his workers' Trust and the staff of two nearby wineries, Ken Forrester and Vriesenhof.

Ilse moved from her administrative and marketing job at Meerlust to take over, assemble a 33-member staff, and build a modern warehouse and bottling facility on a small piece of land. Clients now number 55 producers and they store 2,4 million bottles. The business is healthy. 'We're paying off our R15-million Department of Trade and Industry loan, and though we haven't yet run into enough profits to pay dividends, we're getting there. We're paying our own way with reasonable salaries, building the business, and our provident fund has been able to help some of our bereaved families in need,' says Ilse.

Compagniesdrift recently launched its own wines. The maiden Cabernet-Merlot blend won a silver medal at the 2017 Old Mutual Trophy Wine Show (equivalent to a gold at most other contests). But then the winemaker ('our winemaker', says Ilse) was Chris Williams, in charge of Meerlust's pedigreed lines. 'We're going to appoint an assistant winemaker for Chris, dedicated to our wines,' says Ilse, but they will use Meerlust's facilities.

An unwooded Chardonnay, a Chardonnay-Pinot Noir blend and a dessert Muscat will follow. They're in the very affordable R80–R100 range (terrific value) and now have a listing at airport duty-free shops. 'It's only about 4 000 cases, but still,' Ilse says. 'I don't want to get emotional about this, but this opportunity is really changing our lives.'

Wine, like all agriculture, comprises diverse activities and sometimes long value chains. There are many ways to skin a cat.

Derek Hanekom (centre), Mandela's first Minister of Agriculture and Land Affairs.

FILLING A GAP: NEW SOMMELIERS

The gap was there for the asking. 'Needed,' the ads could have read: 'skilled, informative sommeliers, wine frontline impresarios, charming and fluently conversant but unpretentious, to enhance the fine-dining experience of high-end wine-and-cuisine tourists.'

Until not so very long ago these roles were, with few exceptions, underexploited, and often hopelessly underperformed. As more restaurants upped their game to match Cape Town's growing status as an exceptional international destination, who inserted themselves into these vital Cape wine ambassadorial slots? Zimbabweans, escaping Robert Mugabe's despotic regime.

There are 3–5 million Zimbabweans in South Africa, comprising 5–8% of the population. Some crawled under barbed-wire border fences, cadged lifts in the back of cold bakkies, trains and buses, then fanned across South Africa, to weed gardens, wash bottles or become bartenders.

Immigrant success stories are legion throughout history. They abandon misery at home in search of a better life elsewhere, ready to work hard. In the Zimbabwean case, they're also beneficiaries of a sound basic education at home.

They read up, took exams, tasted and tasted endlessly. Young refugees who had, mostly, never encountered a vine or learned the forbidding art of pairing food and wine. Name any of the restaurants regularly ranked among Cape Town's top dining experiences – The Test Kitchen, La Colombe, Aubergine, Ellerman House, Twelve Apostles, Cape Grace and dozens more – and discover how many professional, confident Zimbabweans are ready to guide you through the imposing wine lists.

There's a cooperative spirit among them. A pernickety German diner is asking for more information on a Riesling pairing at La Colombe, perhaps. Sommelier Tongai Joseph Dhafana, momentarily stuck, WhatsApps the brotherhood; suggestions whizz back; the visitor is placated.

Joseph kicked off the trend for sommeliers to design and market their own wines. The Test Kitchen's Tinashe Nyamudoka and Cape Grace's Marlvin Gwese followed. Pardon Tagazu has assembled an extensive African-wines portfolio for the European market, which includes Ntsiki Biyela's wine.

NO QUICK MONEY

We meet Ntsiki at her old stamping ground at Bosman's Crossing in Stellenbosch, at Pane e Vino, the tiny Italian trattoria run by the Dalla Cia wine-making family. Ntsiki has just returned from a three-week Department of Trade and Industry-funded sales trip to the US, her second, hitting 11 states. Sold out!

Even without a degree, Ntsiki would survive. Anyone who sees *The Colour of Wine* can't but be captivated by this effervescent, indomitable woman with a huge smile, ready to make the most of any moment. She grew up milking cows in the mud, her head resting against a silky warm hide, squirting the odd teatful of milk at anyone around or stealing a mouthful herself. Her mum, a domestic worker, lived away in Durban. 'My grandmother, Aslina, brought me up. She was my everything,' Ntsiki says.

Tinashe Nyamudoka, sommelier at The Test Kitchen in Cape Town.

With the help of Dr Gillian Arendse, her physics lecturer at Stellenbosch University, she overcame a few hiccoughs with the subject – failing it a couple of times – and won her BSc in oenology and viticulture. His grin at tasting her wines – and reading of her successes – is so ecstatic you'd think he'd made the wine himself.

After university, Ntsiki worked as winemaker with Dave and Jane Lello's Stellekaya Winery in Stellenbosch from 2004. Her wines regularly earned four-star ratings in Platter's annual wine guide. In 2014 she branched out on her own, with her Aslina label.

Hers is a multiple balancing act in the ancient art of buying in selected wines and grapes, crafting her own styles and blends for her own labels, and negotiating shipments to outlets, in her case, mostly overseas. 'I'm afloat,' says Ntsiki of her finances. 'But I tell people you mustn't come to this business to make quick money; it's also about life. And I have tons of support.'

In this little corner of Stellenbosch alone, she's had the Lellos and Dalla Cias for help and companionship; and next door is Vilafonté, one of the smartest (red) wines of the Cape, made by winemaker Zelma Long and viticulturist Phil Freese. 'We have to work together; if any one of us puts out dodgy wines, it reflects on all of us,' she says.

> 'We have to work together; if any one of us puts out dodgy wines, it reflects on all of us,' says Ntsiki Biyela.

INDEPENDENT WINEMAKERS

Neil Ellis of Neil Ellis Wines in Stellenbosch is a pioneer in the Cape of Ntsiki's chosen role of independent winemaker and own-label brand marketer. Neil showed from the mid-1980s that a cash-strapped, landless entrepreneur could buy in grapes from anywhere, turn them into fine wines and market them very successfully. It hadn't been done until then – although versions of this expert middleman have been a feature of the traditional wine trade in France for centuries.

Rented space, and winery equipment, were marvels of 'making do' in Neil's earlier years. But he knew a thing or two. One of his first jobs was as cellarmaster at the magisterial Groot Constantia wine estate. And he was daring about locating grapes from obscure vineyards with defining wine personality.

It wasn't until about 30 years later that he invested in a few hectares of vineyards of his own, on the west coast at Darling, and built his own modern winery off the Helshoogte road above Stellenbosch. He's grown it into a family business, with two sons and a daughter, to 100 000 cases (1,2 million bottles) a year.

About mentoring newcomers like Ntsiki he says, 'We haven't scratched the surface; we have to help more.'

If government were to draw more likeminded individuals into the impending big debates on land and the future of wine, they might find they're pushing on open doors.

COMING AND GOING

Mzokhona Mvemve from KwaZulu-Natal was among the first black students to graduate with an oenology and viticulture degree from Stellenbosch University in 1998. He was an early prospect to carry the banner for racial transformation in wine at a senior, authoritative level, and his tasting presentations were superb – detailed and professional. We watched him closely, an industry star in the making.

Dumisani says there are 'many ways
to get into wine', and to transform
Cape wine 'we need to train, but also
to retain. Many qualified young people
have left for other occupations'.

Mzokhona worked his wine practicals at Delaire when Bruwer Raats was winemaker there, and the two forged a bond. They've been in a limited boutique-scale partnership – some 400–500 cases a year – ever since, with an outstanding red. It's a mainly Cabernet-Franc blend from Stellenbosch, called MR de Compostella (for 'Mvemve' and 'Raats'). Raats does the hard slog these days, but they taste together to 'assemble' the blend each vintage – a collectible worth seeking out that's been scoring in the 90–95/100 range from America's two powerful assessment periodicals, *Robert Parker's Wine Advocate* and *Wine Spectator*.

But wine lost Mzo to more lucrative offers in commerce; he's now with South African Breweries in Johannesburg after a long stint in the Eastern Cape. He says he misses the wine business; there's a chuckle but no real regret at not being at the coalface any more. The uncertainties of setting up alone, the cost of gearing up to do it the way he'd prefer, he thinks, are just too onerous when weighed against the security and prospects elsewhere. He believes the government could have done more to support new entrants in wine if it were serious about transformation.

It was difficult at first, says Dumisani Mathonsi, 'getting into the European and French culture of wine. But after a while, it became very easy.' He developed a taste for German Rieslings – 'such romantic, light, aromatic wines' – and New Zealand Sauvignon Blancs – 'they're to die for'. Portuguese Vinho Verdes were another light lunchtime favourite. 'And I used to love Rhone Shiraz blends and Spanish Riojas,' he adds, 'but these days I find reds a bit heavy unless they're well aged.'

It's all some distance from his home near Hluhluwe, in rural KwaZulu-Natal, a wildlife and farming district. Neither of his parents went to school. 'My dad was a steelworker and my mum a housewife.' But his maths and physics were strong enough to win a scholarship to Stellenbosch University. He qualified in 2003 as one of South Africa's first black oenologists, and has this to say: 'That BSc degree is only a ticket for a job; after that there's a whole lot more to learn. Technically you may be a winemaker, but you need to taste carefully, nonstop, to learn to pick up faults, to keep abreast; studying never stops.'

There are 'many ways to get into wine: sommeliers, educators, marketers', he says. To transform Cape wine, 'we need to train, but also to retain. Many qualified young people have left for other occupations'.

He remained at his first job, at Tokara on the Helshoogte Pass above Stellenbosch, for 13 years. He worked under Gyles Webb, one of the most acute wine palates in the Cape, who owns Thelema next door, and Miles Mossop, his immediate boss at Tokara. 'For a few of the early years I was just a glorified cellarworker,' he says.

In 2017 Dumisani accepted a completely different challenge at Distell, also in Stellenbosch, in charge of the Adam Tas cellar, as the white-winemaker. This is a world of giant tanks and clanking machinery echoing around cathedral-sized cellars. In 2018 he crushed 3 000 tons of grapes.

Zonnebloem, one of the oldest top-quality brands, and the more commercial Two Oceans and Drostdy Hof lines are his babies now. 'It's all about careful blending because we haul in grapes from all over,' he says. 'I'm building up my experience.'

He believes wine has a future in black culture: 'You wouldn't believe how enthusiastic people are becoming about it – especially at weddings.' But, he adds, 'the wines need to be branded properly so people feel the labels are relevant and personal to them.'

These stories reflect the diversity of Cape transformation, business models and people. As a group, the projects are still in their formative stages. And they're a small proportion of the 850 producers and brands, only 55 of which are black-owned. Others have foundered, sometimes in acrimony and lack of trust.

Coordinating many of their efforts is none other than Unathi Mantshongo, the viticulturist, now CEO of the VinPro Foundation. Reflecting on Cape wine's future, she's a realist and an optimist. There are 'phenomenal people' among the transformation stake-holders, she says.

As to whether government has played a sufficiently supportive role in the last couple of decades, 'You can't always point a finger at government,' Unathi says. 'The wine-growing/vineyard-farming business is operating at about 1,5% return on capital. Is it a wise investment?' Of government-assisted projects that have foundered, she says, 'I wish they'd come to us first. We could have evaluated the vineyards and prospects properly.'

And of the longer term, Unathi says, 'I'll be long gone before all we need to do here is done.'

'The future of farm workers remains precarious. Increasing mechanisation will cause job losses.'

NO ESCAPING HISTORY

South African wine can't escape its history: the grotesque racial inequalities of apartheid and the legacy of appalling conditions for workers. Peer sanction, in the form of supermarkets and retailers removing wines from shelves, must be used to good effect to discourage practises that perpetuate inequality.

Through initiatives such as Fairtrade Label South Africa (FLSA), Integrated Production of Wine (IPW), and the Wine and Agricultural Ethical Trade Association (WIETA), there are efforts to coordinate and promote ethical labour conditions and sustainable environmental practises. There is an increasing number of charitable events aimed at raising funds for education, most notable of which is the annual Cape Wine Auction, which raised R17 million in 2018. Movers are Wendy Appelbaum of DeMorgenzon and Mike Ratcliffe of Warwick (who sold his estate to American investors in 2018), but dozens of prestigious producers donate the finest, special bottlings in the cause of education. The Cape Winemakers' Guild (CWG) sponsors a Protégé Programme to assist aspiring black winemakers.

However, the future of farm workers remains precarious. Increasing mechanisation will cause job losses. Australia machine-harvests 90% of its wine crop, and South Africa is following at approximately 60%. The Australians prune vines mechanically, too. A couple of families, or a team of five or six, can comfortably harvest and process a 500-ton crop – about 40 000 cases or 480 000 bottles of wine. In the Cape, that would require a staff of 30 or more; a single machine-harvester replaces 40 pickers.

Australia has an official productivity commission to regulate these developments, but there is no sign of this in South Africa. It is little wonder, then, that the consistently first-rate Australian Shiraz has elbowed its way into, and keeps others out of, vast segments of the notoriously difficult Chinese market.

Casualisation has been sweeping labourers off farms for years. Terry Bell, noted political and economic analyst, says trade unions – once strongly established in the form of the Food and Allied Workers' Union (FAWU) – seem to 'have lost their way … with little presence in the winelands. At the bottom of the supply chain is the farmer/worker. The present doesn't look good for the workers.' It's quite different for 'upchain' wine sommeliers: they make more from a tip on a bottle of wine than the farm receives.

These challenges will hasten urbanisation, with two-thirds of South Africa's population already living in urban areas.

Many black workers spend 40% of their salaries on commuting costs. Imaginative planning is necessary to rectify the spatial legacy of apartheid. But time, as widespread protests show, is running out. Soon there will be 40 million urbanites and just 15 million people scattered around South Africa's wide-open spaces.

The land issue remains unresolved, while populist politics and popular frustrations have created a volatile environment in which demands for expropriation without compensation are gaining traction. While new radical policies may promise rapid change, they also threaten the sustainability of an industry that depends on high levels of investment. Some estimates suggest agriculture has incurred in excess of R200 billion in farming bonds.

Both land restitution and land reform programmes are far from complete. The new government in 1994 targeted the transfer of 30% of white-owned farmland to black ownership by 2014. 'Today, in 2018, we're only at 8–10%,' [this refers to land transferred by government] says Professor Ruth Hall of the South African Institute of Land & Agrarian Studies (PLAAS) in Cape Town. Professor Peter Delius, co-author of *Rights to Land*, points out that 19 000 of the original restitution claims have not been finalised, and there are 163 000 new claims in the system which at the current rate of settlements, will take decades to complete.

Meanwhile, the contrast between the sprawling squalor of Khayelitsha when you fly into Cape Town, and the manicured vineyards and grand homesteads you're among twenty minutes down the road, sampling world-class wines, is a potent graphic of the most unequal society in the world.

The road out of Tesselaarsdal.

THE RITUAL OF WINE

'The first thing when you drink wine, is to lift the glass up. Look at the clarity of the wine, then tilt the glass forward a little and analyse the colour and depth. This gives an indication of the grape variety, age and style of winemaking. For example, if it is a white wine, the colour will tell you whether the wine is young or old, dry or sweet (the wine style). A young Sauvignon Blanc will most likely be pale with a green tinge on the edge of the glass. A Chardonnay that was aged in oak barrels will be a light yellow-gold colour. If it is a red wine, a bright red colour will show that the wine is young. Then swirl the wine to break the surface tension, which allows the aromas and flavours to open up so they can be picked up by the nose. Smell the wine to see what odours you pick up. It could be berries, tropical fruits or the spice that comes from oak. There are no wrong or right answers. Sip the wine and swirl it around your mouth to taste the follow-through of the fruit you picked up on the nose. Swallow and enjoy the lingering after-taste.'
— *Dumisani Mathonsi, winemaker*

FOOD AND WINE

NOMPUMELELO MQWEBU

AN AFRICAN CHEF

We don't know each other if we don't know each other's food.

I grew up surrounded by food and great cooks. I was fortunate to be raised by a father who had travelled and worked as a cook on ships. When he was 15 years old, he ran away and boarded a ship, and travelled to far-flung places like Mexico and America. He instilled in us a sense of culinary adventure.

He loved to cook on weekends and there was always something different to look forward to. One night there would be chillies or exotic spices or pickles. And always fish. Lots of delicious fresh fish. He cooked red snapper and sardines freshly caught by fishermen in Margate.

My parents had a shop in Ramsgate, an hour away from where we lived in Umlazi township. During school holidays I would help out. Very early in the morning I would be wrapped in a blanket. We would ride in my dad's old truck, which often wouldn't start, so I had to get out and push. The sun would rise as we travelled the long road to Ramsgate, and my dad would stop at this fish shop and get us fish and chips in newspaper for breakfast. It was a ritual I loved.

In Ramsgate, many people earn their living from the sea. At the end of the day the fishermen would come to the shop and barter with Dad. They exchanged their catch for milk, bread and sometimes chicken. Migrants from Pondoland who worked on the sugarcane farms came for mealie-meal, soap and paraffin.

The fishermen's wives were also regulars. They bought a 'set' to make imfula imfulu (river river), a very potent alcoholic drink. A set consisted of a loaf of brown bread, Jungle Oats, yeast, brown sugar and a pineapple. They would mix it and ferment it. I believe it was very potent but we were never allowed to taste it.

I grew up in the shop, every year getting new responsibilities and learning new skills. I learned to work the till, deal with customers, count the change in plastic packets, and make lists at the end of the day for ordering new supplies.

The other great influence in my culinary life was my Xhosa grandmother. Originally from the Eastern Cape, Noluthando MaGaqa Kunene came to live in KwaZulu-Natal when she was 15 years old and later met and married my grandfather, who was a translator of the court.

She was a real pioneer. In the thick of apartheid she ran a little restaurant, a diner, in Howick. My grandfather would come with his colleagues for lunch. I remember pumpkin pudding and umleqwa (hand-raised) chicken with dumplings – so delicious!

During many school holidays I stayed with my grandmother and worked in the little restaurant, where I got many of my first cooking lessons – and my first burn on a coal stove! I was four years old and jumping on a bench near the stove when I tripped and fell, with both hands landing on the scorching-hot plates. My grandmother bathed my wounds for weeks afterwards. Now, when new chefs get their first kitchen burn, I tell them that I had my first one when I was four years old.

One of the first things my grandmother taught me to cook was porridge. I also helped kneading ujeqe (steamed bread). She taught me not to bang it with my fists but to knead it gently so that it stayed nice and elastic.

Food prepared with love and an open heart always tastes good.

I learned from her that how you treat food matters. Food prepared with love and an open heart always tastes good. And she taught me the importance of growing your own food. At the back of her little Howick house she grew apples, figs, oranges and grapes, and an infinite variety of vegetables. Nothing was wasted. We used peels, grass, eggshell and the like for what I later grew up to discover was to make organic compost. Most fun was to steal fruit from the orchard, which was how I made friends with the neighbouring children.

After matriculating I got a job in Durban working in marketing, then retail. But at the age of 27, I decided to do what I loved most. I resigned and went to cookery school.

Over the next years I worked in different restaurants and, through my own catering company, did birthday parties and weddings. But I hated weddings: the brides always wanted an expensive dress and cheap food. Then in 2006 I got a big break when I was appointed to head the cold kitchen at the upmarket Zimbali Lodge in Ballito Bay. I was thrown in at the deep end but it gave me my grounding.

I've represented South African food at shows in Germany and France and recently won an award in China for my cookbook, *Through the Eyes of an African Chef*, which focuses on African recipes made with indigenous ingredients and skills.

The journey hasn't always been easy. The food business is tough for women. Restaurant kitchens can be crazy places ruled by men who are often rude, aggressive and difficult. It's a workplace where there are lots of knives too! You have to keep your head all the time.

Although I've cooked all around the world – including in New York, London and Paris – my food remains rooted in South Africa. I love to cook with ingredients of local origin like amadumbe (taro root), ubhatat (sweet potato), izindlubu (jugo beans), iselwa (baby pumpkin) and wild berries like amajingijolo (gooseberries). I like to support indigenous farmers and food.

Cooking is a combination of many things – art, science and management. You have to be dexterous and creative. There's nothing to beat the satisfaction of people enjoying your food.

Refiloe Molefe at the Bambanani Food and Herb Cooperative in Bertrams, in Johannesburg's inner city. Refiloe started the gardens in 2006 to provide nutrition for hungry local kids. She leases the land from the City of Johannesburg. Nompumelelo buys her vegetables from the cooperative, and says, 'I'm inspired that Mme Refiloe grew up an orphan and turned her life to giving back and assisting the community. She also has very green fingers! Her veggies are delicious.'

SOUTH COAST SNAPPER *Serves 4*

INGREDIENTS

500g whole red snapper (or similar)
salt to taste
banana leaves

For the stuffing

butter for frying
1 onion, thinly sliced
1 green pepper, deseeded and thinly sliced
10 olives, pitted
turmeric and other fresh herbs to taste
¼ cup chopped parsley
squeeze of lemon juice

METHOD

1. Preheat the oven to 230 °C or prepare a fire for a braai.
2. Scale and gut the fish, and clean with salt water. Dry the surface of the fish using paper (yesterday's newspaper is just fine!).
3. To make the stuffing, fry the onion, green pepper and olives in butter until they're soft and fragrant. Add the turmeric and other fresh herbs and fry for a few minutes more. Remove from the heat and add the parsley and lemon juice.
4. Using a sharp knife, make shallow incisions about 2,5cm apart on both sides of the fish. Rub the fish with salt to taste.
5. Spoon the stuffing into the fish, then wrap the fish with banana leaves.
6. Place the fish in the oven or over the coals. Turn after 10 minutes, then cook for a further 10–15 minutes.
7. Serve on a bed of lightly fried shaved courgettes and top with pickled red onion.

AMADUMBE GNOCCHI

WITH FILLET & CHARRED VEGETABLES

INGREDIENTS

800g amadumbe (taro roots), unpeeled, cut into cubes
salt and pepper to taste
300g flour (and some extra to dust the gnocchi)
1 egg
4 x 250–300g beef fillets
olive oil
½ teaspoon wholegrain mustard
1–2 sprigs of thyme and rosemary
4 miniature corn on the cob
4 small carrots
2 red bell peppers
basil leaves to garnish
sea salt

For the cheese sauce
50g butter
1 clove garlic (chopped into a paste)
50g flour
750ml milk
¼ teaspoon nutmeg
salt and pepper to taste
20g Gorgonzola cheese

METHOD

1. In a large pot, boil the amadumbe in salted water to cover until soft (15–20 minutes). Drain, peel and mash while still warm, then squeeze through a sieve.

2. On a floured countertop, mix amadumbe, salt and pepper and flour, forming a mound. Make a well in the centre and crack the egg into it. Use a fork to combine, then use your fingertips to bring it all together to form a dough. Avoid adding too much flour and over-kneading. Shape into a wide rectangle about 25cm long. Cut lengthwise into 10 pieces. Roll each long piece into 2,5cm sections using a sharp knife or pastry cutter to smooth out the roll. Put in a cool dry area for at least 4–5 hours, preferably overnight. Depending on the humidity levels where you live, you may need to turn the gnocchi to ensure they dry on both sides.

3. Preheat the oven to 200 °C.

4. Make a rub for the fillets by combining the olive oil, mustard and seasoning to taste. Rub all over the fillets and set aside.

5. To make the sauce, melt the butter over low heat in a medium-sized thick-based saucepan. Add the garlic, then slowly whisk in the flour until the roux has a cookie smell. Slowly whisk in the milk while cooking. Season with nutmeg, salt and pepper. Add the Gorgonzola cheese and cook for a further 5 minutes.

6. Gently shake any excess flour off the gnocchi. Cook the gnocchi in a large pot of salted boiling water for 2–4 minutes. They will float to the top when ready. Remove with a slotted spoon and toss in a large saucepan with the sauce for 2 minutes.

7. Sear the meat in a very hot pan, browning all sides, then place on an oven tray. Reduce the oven temperature to 180 °C and bake the fillet to preferred state of readiness (rare 2½ minutes per side, medium-rare 3–4 minutes per side, medium 3½–5 minutes per side).

8. Sprinkle sea salt over the mealies, carrots and bell peppers. Place on the griddle and turn gently with tongs as they cook. Remove once lightly charred, not burned!

9. Plate the vegetables, slice and stack the fillet onto the vegetables, and smother liberally with gnocchi and cheese sauce.

UMKANTSHA

SAMP AND BEANS IN MARROW BONES

INGREDIENTS

2 cups samp (coarse corn kernels)
300g marrow bones
1 medium-sized onion, diced
3 litres vegetable, chicken or beef stock
1 cup sugar beans
salt to taste
knob of butter

METHOD

1. Rinse the samp in cold water, then soak overnight in just enough hot water to cover.
2. Preheat the oven to 180 °C. Place the marrow bones and onion on a baking tray and brown in the oven for 15 minutes. Remove roasted marrow from a couple of bones and set aside for garnish.
3. In a medium-sized pot, place the samp with its liquid, the bones and 2 litres of the stock, and cook for 15 minutes from cold.
4. Stirring, add the beans and the rest of the stock, and cook for a further 40 minutes on low heat or until the mixture is soft enough according to your preference – the samp and beans should be soft and the remaining marrow should have fallen off the bone and into the samp. Add more water if necessary for longer cooking time. Season with salt. Remove and set aside the bones.
5. For richer flavour, add the knob of butter just before serving.
6. Serve in a small bowl, or in the reserved marrow bones, cutting them lengthways. Garnish with the roasted marrow.

ISIJINGI

PUMPKIN PUDDING

INGREDIENTS

400g pumpkin or butternut, peeled and cubed
120g maizemeal
15g butter
250ml cream
2,5ml ground cinnamon
sugar or honey to taste
fresh mixed berries to serve

METHOD

1. Cook the pumpkin/butternut in water to cover until soft enough to mash, ensuring you have enough water to reserve 2 cups. Strain and reserve the water.
2. Purée the pumpkin/butternut in a blender, gradually adding the reserved water.
3. Place the purée in a pot on medium heat. When it comes to the boil, whisk in the maizemeal. Slowly stir in the butter, cream and cinnamon. Cook for about 15 minutes. Add sugar or honey to taste.
4. Pour into ramekins and garnish with fresh berries to serve.

SOMMELIER

BONGANI NGWENYA

A SOMMELIER'S JOURNEY

It was a big step from the dusty streets of Newcastle to tasting wines in the Cape. I was doing presentations for international clientele, selling a product I'd never heard of where I grew up.

I was born in Newcastle in KwaZulu-Natal. It's a small town with few employment opportunities. We were seven children raised by my mom who worked as a domestic worker. Financially, things were tough.

After I finished school I left Newcastle to look for work. A friend who'd got a job at Spier Wine Farm called me and suggested that I join him. He said there were better opportunities in the Cape than in Newcastle. So a month later I got on a train and headed for Stellenbosch. It was the longest train ride I'd ever taken in my life: I had to travel from Newcastle to Johannesburg and from Johannesburg to Cape Town. That was 1996.

When I arrived in Stellenbosch I'd never seen such lush green vineyards or oak-shaded streets with so many restaurants before.

My friend introduced me to this guy who was the stable manager at the Spier Equestrian Centre. For six months, I groomed and fed horses, cleaned the stables and managed pony rides for children.

Then I thought that rather than cleaning stables, I would clean the Wine Centre. It was probably a bit more hygienic! That's where my wine-career journey started.

I had to mop the floor, clean the toilets and wash the glasses. But I would listen to the talks and I became curious. People talked of wine being 'dry'. And I asked myself, *How can it be dry when it's a liquid?* And people said it was 'fruity', and I wondered where that came from. I started asking questions, reading wine magazines and tasting wine. At first I drank wines that were semi-sweet, which I really enjoyed.

My boss at the Wine Centre, Jabulani Ntshangase, called me aside and said that the only way to succeed in life is to be the best at whatever you do: 'You're the cleaner – be the best cleaner that this company has ever had.' So I took that advice. My working day was from 9am to 5pm. But I would come in at 7am and finish most of my cleaning duties so that by 9am, when I was supposed to start, I'd done almost all my work. Then I used the time to ask questions and get more information about what went on in the Wine Centre.

The management at Spier could see I was hungry for knowledge and it was then that I got my first big chance, when they offered me the opportunity to go to the Cape Wine Academy and do a one-week introductory course on South African wines.

After the course I became a trainee wine merchant. I still had cleaning duties but helped with stocktaking and wine sales in the shop. Then I began to present wine tastings at the centre. It was a big step from the dusty streets of Newcastle. I was doing presentations for international clientele, selling a product I'd never heard of where I grew up.

I never stopped studying. In 2006 I did a two-year wine-management programme at Stellenbosch University Business School. I learned about wine marketing and business management. The course was tough. I'd never been exposed to the business world before. It was all new to me, and the other students were mostly Afrikaans-speaking. But while I was there I was given an incredible opportunity to go to the USA to learn about wines of the world and to promote South African wine. It was there that I heard the word 'sommelier' for the first time. I didn't know what a sommelier was but I knew I'd found what I wanted to do.

That was in 1997 and there were no courses in South Africa where you could train to be a sommelier. But I got my first job at Bosman's Restaurant at the Grande Roche Hotel in the Paarl winelands and they trained me on the job. I started as a junior and moved up to be assistant sommelier. I learned about decanting, how to serve wines and when to use different glassware. I loved it!

Over the next few years I worked at different restaurants and hotel groups, learning and gaining experience as an assistant food and beverage manager, and then as a sommelier.

In 2016 I started at The Codfather in Sandton, where I still am today. My job is varied and exciting. Among other things, I have to source the wine for the restaurant. I don't just order wines I like – I have to be able to sell them, so I need to know what the latest trends are and what wines are selling. From this I create a wine list.

The menu changes seasonally – the food we serve in winter is different to our summer menu – so when the chef is creating new dishes, I participate, taste and suggest wines to go with the new dish. I also do staff training because it's important that our waiters know and understand the wines that they're serving.

When it comes to pairing, I always try to find out what customers enjoy, then I can suggest something to them.

I'm a part-time facilitator for the sommelier academy of the Gauteng Department of Tourism Internship Programme. It seeks to bring young people from previously disadvantaged backgrounds into the wine world. I teach the winemaking component to young people studying to be sommeliers. Most students who come on the course are unemployed at the time of signing up but have expressed an interest in the industry. Students are placed in restaurants or hotels where they do their practicals. Many students are starting out on the same journey as I did. Wine wasn't something they were exposed to when they grew up. It's a new world for them, just as it was for me 22 years ago when I first started cleaning the floors at Spier.

Marsel Janse van Rensburg, head chef at The Codfather in Johannesburg, where he and Bongani plan menus and wine pairings.

CAJUN SEARED SALMON

Serves 4

WITH PICKLED ONION AND TERIYAKI SAUCE

INGREDIENTS

4 x 120g pieces of salmon
salt and pepper to taste
20g Cajun spice
50g butter
50ml olive oil
125ml teriyaki sauce

Onion pickle
125ml vinegar
125ml mirin
2 bay leaves
1 red onion

METHOD

1. To make the pickle, put the vinegar, mirin and bay leaves into a pot and bring to the boil. Let it simmer for 5 minutes, then remove from the heat. Thinly slice the red onion and add to the liquid. Refrigerate for at least a day so that the onion becomes soft.
2. Warm up a frying pan or griller. Add 30g butter and 30ml olive oil. Place two pieces of salmon, skin-side down, and fry for 2 or 3 minutes to get the skin crispy. Turn the salmon over and cook for 1 minute on the other side. Then cook for 1 minute further on each side. Pour the olive oil/butter mixture over the fish while cooking to give the fish flavour. Remove the fish from the pan, season with salt and pepper and Cajun spice, and keep warm. Add the rest of the butter and olive oil to the pan, and repeat with the other two pieces of salmon.
3. To serve, spread some onion pickle on each plate and place the salmon on top. Serve the teriyaki sauce in a bowl on the side.

'Pinot Noir is the ideal wine with salmon. The light red fruits and earthy, savoury nature of a Pinot are a perfect match for the rich and savoury meat of the salmon. Salmon is an oily fish, and Pinot has a medium acidity, which cuts through and balances the dish's oiliness.'
— Bongani Ngwenya, sommelier

MUSSEL AND PRAWN CHOWDER

Serves 4

INGREDIENTS

400g fresh mussels
8 fresh prawns
1 large carrot, peeled and chopped
1 potato, peeled and chopped
1 small onion, peeled and chopped
2 sticks celery, chopped
2 cloves garlic, crushed
oil for frying
80g butter
80ml vegetable stock
80ml fish stock
350ml fresh cream
salt and pepper to taste
fresh thyme, basil and dill to taste

METHOD

1. Boil mussels for 1 minute to open the shells; throw away any that don't open. Remove the flesh and roughly chop it.
2. Remove and discard the heads and tails of the prawns, and take out the black vein in the middle. Cut in half lengthwise, and then in half across.
3. Fry the carrot, potato, onion, celery and garlic in a little oil until golden-brown. Add the mussels and prawns and fry until the prawns turn pink.
4. In a separate pan, add the butter, vegetable and fish stock, and cream. Bring to the boil and simmer for about 5 minutes. Add the thyme, basil and dill just before serving.

'This seafood dish is rich and creamy. I think it needs a wine with body and energy that complements the creamy, buttery flavour of the food. A South African Chardonnay would be delicious with this recipe.'
— Bongani Ngwenya, sommelier

GRILLED RED ROMAN

Serves 4

WITH CREAMY SAFFRON AND HERB SAUCE

INGREDIENTS
200g French beans, topped and tailed
4 new potatoes, halved
30ml olive oil
fresh thyme and rosemary to taste
knob of salted butter
4 x 180g red roman
salt and pepper to taste

Basil pesto
300g fresh basil
2 cloves garlic, crushed
½ cup Parmesan cheese
60ml lemon juice
80ml olive oil
salt and pepper to taste

Saffron sauce
30g butter
50ml vegetable stock
generous pinch of saffron
20ml lemon juice
125ml fresh cream
salt and pepper to taste

METHOD
1. To make the basil pesto, blend the basil, garlic, Parmesan, lemon juice, olive oil and salt and pepper to make a smooth paste.
2. To make the saffron sauce, melt the butter, then add the vegetable stock, saffron, lemon juice and cream. Let it reduce, then add salt and pepper to taste.
3. Blanch the beans for 3 minutes, then put them in iced water to stop the cooking process. Boil the potatoes until just done. Combine the potatoes and beans with the olive oil and sauté together for about 3 minutes. Add thyme and rosemary. Just before serving add a knob of salted butter to give it creaminess.
4. Grill the fish with seasoning for 3 minutes on each side until golden-brown.
5. To serve, put the beans and potatoes on a plate, and place the red roman on top. Drizzle over saffron sauce and basil pesto.

'Saffron is an amazing spice to pair with wine. Saffron adds depth to this dish by creating intense aromas and adds a slight bitterness to the sweetness. Sauvignon Blanc is a fruitier wine with a crisp and zingy finish, and is a great wine with this dish.'
— Bongani Ngwenya, sommelier

SITHEMBISO MTHETHWA

GETTING AWAY FROM THE NOISE

We live in a world full of noise. Cooking helps me get away from it all.

We live in a world where everything is rushed and cooking helps get me into the slow lane. I love the creative challenge of cooking a meal for family and friends. Unlike long-term investment feedback, with cooking I get to realise the outcome of my efforts within hours. I get the opportunity to put theory to the test.

I recently discovered rabbit meat and I love cooking it. It's simple to prepare and is just delicious. It's estimated that there are 200 rabbit farmers in South Africa, currently geared for export. However, rabbit meat will soon be stocked in supermarkets around the country.

RABBIT STEW

INGREDIENTS

zest of 1 lemon

90ml olive oil

salt and pepper to taste

8 rabbit legs (or chicken legs)

¼ cup flour

¼ cup onion, finely diced

4 cloves garlic, minced

8 button mushrooms, quartered

1 large carrot, chopped

8 small potatoes, quartered

4 radishes, quartered

1 teaspoon dried thyme

1 sprig fresh origanum, minced

½ bottle white wine (I use Pinot Grigio)

about 2 cups chicken stock

salt and pepper to taste

METHOD

1. Combine the lemon zest, 60ml olive oil and seasoning. Coat the rabbit legs with this mixture, and set aside.
2. Heat a large heavy-bottomed pot over medium-high heat and coat the bottom with 30ml olive oil. Dust the rabbit legs with flour, shaking off any excess, and cook on both sides until browned, about 5 minutes. Set aside.
3. Add the onion and garlic to the pan, and sauté for 1 minute. Add the mushrooms, carrot, potatoes, radishes, thyme and half the origanum. Sauté for 3 minutes or until beginning to brown.
4. Add the white wine, scraping up any bits that may have stuck to the bottom of the pot.
5. Return the rabbit to the pot. Add enough chicken stock to just cover the rabbit.
6. Cover and simmer for 45 minutes to 1 hour or until the rabbit is tender.
7. Remove the rabbit legs and reduce the sauce by half.
8. Return the rabbit to the sauce and serve with fresh buttered bread.

'Rabbit has a very high protein content and very low fat content. Rabbit goes really well with the intense freshness of Sauvignon Blanc and in the company of good friends.'

SUZAAN HAUPTFLEISCH

SOUTH AFRICAN FOOD & WINE IN NEW YORK CITY

Kaia Wine Bar and Restaurant has 60–70 wines by the glass because I want the most wines from South Africa to hit the most American palates. That is how I like to drink. I like to try different things. I want New Yorkers to taste a whole range of South African wines.

I grew up on a farm and in a country where you can just get in your car, drive to a friend's house unannounced with a bottle of wine, and have the best time. That is what South Africa is to me and I created an environment at Kaia where people can walk in without a reservation, eat our food and drink our country's wine.

We're supported and loved by our local Upper East Side neighborhood, but it's still difficult to get support from the South African wine industry, that has not quite figured out how to sell our country's wine to Americans. After eight years of owning a successful restaurant, I think I have proven that South African wine is a hot commodity.

Kaia's concept is perfect for our times, where restaurants are leaning toward a more casual approach versus that of white tablecloth service. Millennials, who are often overlooked in our wine industry, appreciate this more casual intimacy with food and wine. They travel more than their parents did, visit more unchartered wine territories like South Africa, and spend more than previous generations on food, experiences, travel and wine. I want everyone who makes an effort to spend money at Kaia to know I appreciate them. They bring their willingness and wallets to the table, and we're in a position to educate newcomers to South African wine or re-introduce older palates to the new wave of quality South African producers.

For me, South African cooking and our spices invoke food memories that are warm, homey and familiar. It is that stacked Sunday lunch table on our farm, with my mom and gran's food and desserts like yskastert (fridge tart), malva pudding, afval (tripe), tamatiekos (lamb tomato stew), curries, homemade breads, jellies and jams. And in the summer, canning! My best memories are those beautiful Free State afternoons spent around vats of apricots, peaches and turksvye (prickly pears), preparing them for canning. We ate what the land gave us, and it is those memories that I use as my compass at Kaia.

I change Kaia's food menu once every four months, with the seasons. Some of the favorites on our menu stay year-round, like the rooibos tea and cranberry babyback pork ribs, which is a staple I never take off the menu. Our lamb burger with chef Billy Dineen's sour cherry compote, Roquefort cheese and pickled cucumbers on brioche is very popular, and he makes delicious spicy octopus tentacles with a fresh seasonal salad and Cape gooseberries.

What I love about Kaia is that people who visit the restaurant know that we are South African. They come specifically to eat and experience our kind of food and spices, and drink our country's wine. I also try to stock as many older vintages on our wine list as I can find. We have regulars that come in just to drink those rare older vintages. I also try to carry a wide representation of all of our wine regions, like Elgin, Breedekloof, and areas like the Swartland. Most importantly, I try to have as many South African female winemakers and winemakers of colour on our list. The American wine drinker is turning to more sustainably produced wines, with little or no interference.

My staff are well versed in our country's wines and equipped to pair our wines with our food, although we generally prefer not to dictate what someone might enjoy. There are no hard rules for me with wine, as long as I achieve my goal of introducing our brilliant wine talent to America. We love throwing wine dinners at Kaia, where we feature amazing talents like Ntsiki Biyela, who I met about nine years ago in Stellenbosch. Our wine events sell out regularly, and our guests get the opportunity to meet the winemaker when they come to town and drink as much of their wine as they want. Chef Billy loves to create menus inspired by the winemaker's background, wine and country. We've had a few events with Ntsiki, and recently Chef Billy created a Zulu-themed dinner to celebrate Ntsiki and to pair with her delicious wines. It was wonderful to build context to her wines with food, and bring it to an American audience.

Ultimately, providing context to wine with food is the only way we are going to succeed as a South African wine industry in the USA. In New York City, you find many French, Italian and Spanish restaurants and that is why their wines out-sell ours. I believe the more Kaias there are in the US, the better for South African wine.

'What I love about Kaia is that people who visit the restaurant know that we are South African.'

FLORENCE FABRICANT

NO RULES TO TASTE

People who work in food and wine are extremely passionate about what they do. They're not in it just to make money.

Wine is extremely tolerant, and if you enjoy the wine you're drinking and you enjoy the food you're eating, it's not often you'll make a huge mistake.

There are not a lot of rules around pairing. Most people will want red wine with their cheese. I don't. I believe white wine is a much better choice because the acidity is a way of balancing the amount of fat in the cheese. The salt that you often have in the cheese is better with a white wine.

Sometimes I like to address a mood when I'm selecting a wine. Or it's the weather. On a hot summer's night, you might want something lighter and cooler. At the same time, something cold and refreshing may not be the thing on a freezing winter's night.

I tell people, 'If you're new to drinking wine, write down the names of the wines you like. Go to a good wine shop and follow their advice. If you like what you bought, drink it again.' Gradually you'll build a palate and form your own taste. Gradually you'll go from simpler wine to wines with more complexity.

But I also tell people not to be afraid to order the cheapest wine on the list because it can be very good. And don't be afraid to order an unfamiliar wine. What do you have to lose?

The big challenge for South African wine is the fact that no one in the USA knows anything about South African food. And if you go into an Italian restaurant, you look for an Italian wine. You go to a French restaurant and see French wines. But there are very few African restaurants in New York. So to sell South African wines abroad, you have to make a real effort with restaurants and sommeliers.

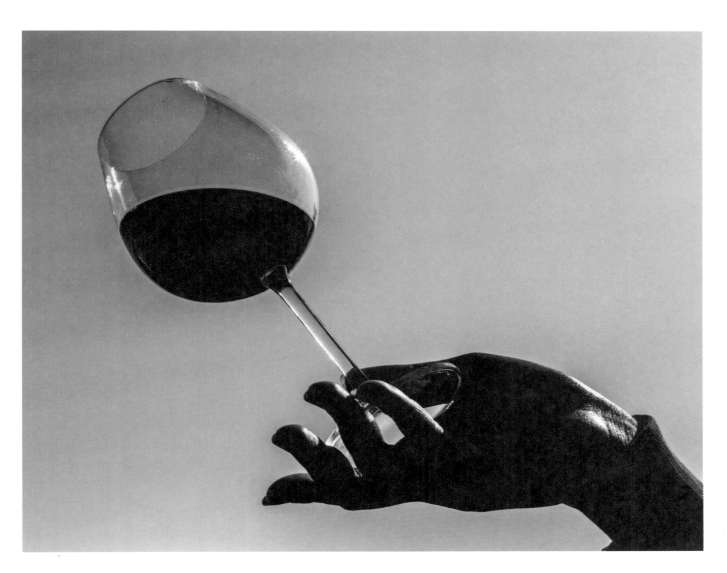

'I remember the first time I tasted wine. It was in Kenya and we would often have it for picnics. The way we drank it wasn't out of glasses or anything. We would just hand the carafe around. You held it up to your mouth and drank and got this big rush of flavours. It hit all your senses in one big go. It was fantastic!'
— John Platter, wine writer

FOOD AND WINE

'At wine shows I am often asked about food and wine pairing. What does that mean? People say "Does that mean I must buy oysters to go with this wine?" I say no. I remember one night I had a bottle of Merlot in the house. I was cooking at home and decided to make my grandmother's chicken curry with masala powder. I made the chicken, some pap and opened the bottle of Merlot. I was in shock! I had been told that spicy food doesn't go with red wine. I phoned my friend and said, "You won't believe it. I'm eating chicken curry and drinking Merlot and they're delicious together." So open a bottle of wine and cook what you want to eat, because at the end of the day it's about what you enjoy. A good meal is about everything that goes with the meal: food, wine, the surroundings, family and friends.'

— *Ntsiki Biyela, winemaker*

ACKNOWLEDGEMENTS

The Colour of Wine documentary film and book was made possible with funding from the Kalipha Foundation of Mion Holdings. We owe a great debt of gratitude for the generous support.

This book was born out of the documentary film of the same name, that premiered at the iREP International Documentary Film Festival in Lagos in March 2018. The film has since been viewed at international festivals and in cinemas in South Africa. It's available online and as a DVD with this book.

Making a documentary is a long journey, with many twists, turns and surprises along the way. First thanks go to Sithembiso Mthethwa and Manana Nhlanhla – founding members and directors of the Kalipha Foundation – who not only supported the film but also came up with the idea to do a book. It is rare to find such generous support – both financial and creative. They travelled the road with us, never balking at our often-crazy requests, helped to shape the content of the book, and provided insights and encouragement.

Thanks to Victor Dlamini who brought the project to director Akin Omotoso, who in turn invited me to join him and producer Rethabile Molatela Mothobi, as a co-producer and co-writer on the film.

Most of the characters in this book appear in the film. Their stories were gathered in interviews conducted by myself and Akin. Hours and hours of interviews with more than 40 people were transcribed, listened to and edited. The results bear testimony to the richness of these stories and Akin's remarkable skill as a director and storyteller.

For the book, I conducted additional interviews, which I transcribed and edited. Others came on board to reshape interviews, conduct new ones and write additional stories. Thanks to Sharon Cort, Wesley Thompson, Jaci de Villiers, Michelle Hay, Michael Fridjhon and John Platter.

Special thanks go to Mark Lewis, the photo editor and primary photographer, who painstakingly selected each and every photograph for this book, ensuring that the images inspire the reader to see a world they thought they knew or didn't know, afresh. The photographs for Bongani Ngwenya and Marsel Janse van Rensburg's recipes were shot at The Codfather restaurant in Sandton, with special thanks to owner, George Sinovich. The photographs for Nompumelelo Mqwebu's recipes were shot at BlackOlive House in Maboneng, with thanks to Nonhlanhla Masombuka. Thanks to Oldenburg Vineyards where the photographs on pages 47, 52 and 54 were taken, and to Summerhill Winery where we took the photographs on page 49.

Thank you to Russell Clarke at Bookstorm whose eye for detail, enthusiasm and support kept me focused and sane enough to complete this book in record time. Thanks to Tracey Hawthorne and Wesley Thompson for great editing, and René de Wet for your exquisite design. Thanks too to Nicola van Rooyen and Erika Walker at Bookstorm, and Prathisha Arjoon at Mion Holdings for your consistent support.

Sithembiso Mthethwa and Manana Nhlanhla, founding members and directors of the Kalipha Foundation of Mion Holdings.

A special thanks to Peter Delius for reading many drafts, making endless cups of much-needed coffee, and for support, always.

Finally, when I began working on *The Colour of Wine* I was an enthusiastic wine drinker who enjoyed wine with family and friends. But my knowledge of the wine industry was rudimentary to say the least. I certainly didn't know the difference between viticulture and oenology! But I learned quickly from the people I met, who generously gave their time. Special thanks to Ntsiki Biyela, Dumisani Mathonsi, Carmen Stevens, Gillian Arendse, Jabulani Ntshangase, Bongani Ngwenya, Michael Fridjhon, Jan Theron, Erna Blancquaert, Philip Costandius, Unathi Mantshongo and John Platter for replying to my endless calls and emails, answering my interminable questions and patiently explaining the world of wine to me. What a gift to have had you all as my teachers.

Harriet Perlman
Johannesburg